1850

MW00860737

N INDOLOGY

MOTILAL BANARSIDASS PUBLISHERS
DELHI

2003

NARSIDASS

SHERS

THE QURANIC SUFISM

The Quranic Sufism

Mir Valiuddin

MOTILAL BANARSIDASS PUBLISHERS
PRIVATE LIMITED • DELHI

First Published: 1959
Second Revised Edition: 1977
Reprint: 1987, 2002

ISBN: 81-208-0320-5

Also available at:
MOTILAL BANARSIDASS
41 U.A. Bungalow Road, Jawahar Nagar, Delhi 110 007
8 Mahalaxmi Chamber, 22 Bhulabhai Desai Road, Mumbai 400 026
120 Royapettah High Road, Mylapore, Chennai 600 004
236, 9th Main III Block, Jayanagar, Bangalore 560 011
Sanas Plaza, 1302 Baji Rao Road, Pune 411 002
8 Camac Street, Kolkata 700 017
Ashok Rajpath, Patna 800 004
Chowk, Varanasi 221 001

Printed in India
BY JAINENDRA PRAKASH JAIN AT SHRI JAINENDRA PRESS,
A-45 NARAINA, PHASE-I, NEW DELHI 110 028
AND PUBLISHED BY NARENDRA PRAKASH JAIN FOR
MOTILAL BANARSIDASS PUBLISHERS PRIVATE LIMITED,
BUNGALOW ROAD, DELHI 110 007

FOREWORD

Sufism or Tasawwuf is variously defined. But whatever the variations in definition, its essential role, as recognised on all hands, is to set in motion a process of spiritual culture, operating in one form or another, for spiritual tranquillity. The mystic tendency in human nature which Tasawwuf treats of has been characteristic of serious minds in all ages and among every section of humanity. The experience in individual cases has varied, both in scope and intensity, according to the vision caught of the Ground of things in life. Indeed long before the advent of Islam, it had been subjected to a searching analysis particularly in societies given to metaphysical speculation such as the Greeks and the ancient Indo-Aryans, and reduced to a system of spiritual training.

Mysticism as practised by the followers of Islam has had a chequered history. In its earliest manifestation, it meant nothing but living from moment to moment, so to say, in the eyes of God, implicitly following the lines of thought and conduct as the Prophet had laid both for himself and his followers. The primary aim was to transform every spiritual flight in the realm of self-perfection into an urge for the spiritual perfection of human society at large. But as Islam expanded into a widening political power, drawing into its fold people born to other modes of life and thought, the mystic tendency among Muslims underwent a kaleidoscopic change. The change was marked by the rise of a bewildering variety of mystic schools influenced chiefly by the Neo-platonism of Alexandria and the Vedantism of India, promoting in the mystic mind the mood for self-negation. A feeling of alarm was therefore felt in serious minds. As a way out, attempts were made at important stages in the history of Sufism to reconcile the early approach to the new forces at work. But the purists among the Sufis, though resolved into several orders themselves by the pressure of time and factors of geography, and though unable to dispense altogether with the terminology of the innovating heterodox schools, have struggled hard to keep to the original way of thought and living. It is the ideology of these and their practices which form the subject of this monograph.

The task, it may be observed, has been discharged not by a student of research interested in the subject only at the intellectual plane, but by a scholar who is not only an ardent believer in the ideology, but who has tried to practise it in his own personal life. As a student of philosophy and as a professor of that subject for years at the Osmania University, it was open to Dr. Mir Valiuddin to have spread the subject on a wide metaphysical canvas and instituted comparisons. He has, however, very rightly confined himself to presenting the view, as it has appeared to him, of the mystic heritage which, undisturbed by the disturbance of history, has continued from the earliest times to mould and shape the life of many a godly man and woman in Islam.

The work is intended to present, what the author believes to be, the contribution of the Quran to Mysticism, and has therefore a value to all seekers of knowledge on that subject.

SYED ABDUL LATIF

CONTENTS

ACKNOWLEDGEMENTS

While issuing this volume, I consider it my duty to acknowledge certain obligations. In the first place, my thanks are due to the Academy of Islamic Studies, Hyderabad and to its distinguished President, Dr. Syed Abdul Latif, for the honour they have done me by according to my monograph a place in their series of learned publications. The index to the volume has been prepared by two of my colleagues at the Osmania University—Dr. Yousufuddin, M. A., PH. D. (Osm.), Reader, Department of Religion and Culture, and Dr. A. N. Khalidi, M. A., D. LITT. (Cairo), Reader in History. I take this occasion to offer them my thanks. My thanks are also due to Messrs Motilal Banarsidass of Delhi for the kindly manner in which they undertook the task of printing the work at their own cost. Notwithstanding the care taken by them in executing the work, a few typographical errors have crept in which the indulgent reader may generously condone.

MIR VALIUDDIN

CHAPTER I

INTRODUCTION

What is Ṣūfism ?

Scholars wrangle about the derivation of the word Ṣūfī, though about its exact connotation I do not think that there is any reason to quarrel Let us cast a hurried glance at the various attempts of the lexicographers:[1]

1. Some say: "The Ṣūfīs were only named Ṣūfīs because of the purity (Ṣāfā) of their hearts and the cleanliness of their acts (āthār)." Bishr ibn al-Ḥārith said: "The Ṣūfī is he whose heart is sincere (Ṣāfā) towards God." Another great Ṣūfī has said: "The Ṣūfī is he whose conduct towards God is sincere, and towards whom God's blessing is sincere." It is evident that the whole body is reformed and all actions improved by purity and sincerity of heart. The unveiling of divine gnosis is entirely dependent on inner purity. As the Prophet said:[2]

"Mark, in man there is a lump of flesh, if it is kept wholesome the whole body remains in a healthy condition and if it is corrupted, the whole body is corrupted, mark, it is the heart!" (Bukhārī)

But if the term Ṣūfī were derived from "Ṣafā" the correct form would be 'Safawī' and not Ṣūfī.

2. Others think that the Ṣūfīs were called Ṣūfīs only "because they are in the first rank (Ṣaff) before God, through the elevation of their desires towards Him, the turning of their hearts unto Him and the staying of their secret parts before Him."

But if the term Ṣūfī were referred to Ṣaff (rank) it would be Ṣaffī and not Ṣūfī.

3. Others have said: "They were called Ṣūfīs because their qualities resembled those of the people of the Bench (Aṣḥab al-Ṣuffā) who lived in the time of God's Prophet. They had left this world, departed from their homes and fled from their companions. They took of this world's good only so much as

was indispensable for covering the nakedness and allaying hunger." One of them was asked: "Who is a Ṣūfī?" He replied: "He who neither possesses nor is possessed." By this he meant that he is not the slave of desires. Another said: "The Ṣūfī is he who possesses nothing, or if he possesses anything spends it."

But if the term Ṣūfī were derived from 'Ṣūffah' (or Bench) the correct form would be "Ṣūffī" and not Ṣūfī!

4. Lastly it has been claimed that they were only called Ṣūfīs because of their habit of wearing Ṣūf, i.e. wool. "For they did not put on raiment soft to touch or beautiful to behold, to give delight to the soul. They only clothed themselves to hide their nakedness contenting with rough-hair cloth and coarse wool."

If the derivation from Ṣūf (wool) be accepted the word is correct and the expression sound from the etymological point of view. According to Arabic lexicon the word "Taṣawwafā" means "he donned woollen dress", as for instance, 'taqammasā' means 'he put on a shirt'. Abū Bakr al-Kalābadhī thinks that the word Ṣūfī "at the same time has all the necessary meanings such as withdrawal from the world, inclining the soul away from it, leaving all settled abodes, keeping constantly to travel, denying the soul its carnal pleasures, purifying the conduct, cleansing the conscience, dilation of the breast, and the quality of leadership."[3]

Ibn Khaldūn was also of the opinion that the word Ṣūfī is derived from Ṣūf. But it is necessary to remember that it is not merely by putting on rough hair-cloth and coarse wool that one is called a Ṣūfī. As Hujwirī has said: "Purity (Ṣafā) is a blessing from God and the 'wool' (Ṣūf) is a proper dress of the cattle."[4]

According to the researches of Imām Qushayrī the word "Ṣūfī" came into vogue a little before the expiry of the second century Hijri (or 822 A.D.). After the death of the Holy Prophet[5], "Companions" was the title adopted by the people of that age. They needed no better title, for "Companionship" was unanimously regarded to be the highest and the best.[6] Those who associated with the "Companion" were called in their own times Tābe' yīn (Followers). And "The followers of the followers"[7] was the title conferred upon those who sat at the feet of the Followers. After the expiry of this period there was a slackening of religious spirit. Hearts were turning more towards the pleasures of the world than towards God. A number of systems and orders cropped up. Each order was divided into a number of branches. Seeing this state of affairs those who adored God above all things and were wholly consumed by the fire of His love, separated themselves from the rest of the world and devoted themselves to the recollection and remembrance of God—the only object of their love. These men were later called the "Ṣūfīs." They were cut off from the mundane world for God's sake—clean of impurities, full of meditations, in their eyes gold and mud were of equal value. And that is why Abū Ali al-Rūdhbārī has defined a Ṣūfī thus:[8]

"One who wears wool over (his) purity, gives his lusts the taste of tyranny, and having overthrown the world, journeys in the pathway of the chosen one" (i.e. the Prophet).[9]

In the light of these historical facts it is now easy to determine the exact meaning of Ṣūfīsm. If you cast a glance over the various definitions of Ṣūfīsm given by the Ṣūfīs themselves you will find not a few necessary attributes ascribed to them. It is not necessary to try to state them all here. But the gist of them all is beautifully expressed in a definition formulated by Shaykh-al-Islām Zakariyah Anṣārī, which is as follows:[10]

"Ṣūfīsm teaches how to purify one's self, improve one's morals, and build up one's inner and outer life in order to attain perpetual bliss. Its subject matter is the purification of the soul and its end or aim is the attainment of eternal felicity and blessedness."

The following few sayings of the more prominent Ṣūfīs amplify and extend with fresh details the definition above formulated:

Imām Qushayrī, the author of the great Ṣūfī compendium Rasā'il, takes Ṣūfism in the sense of purity (safā), i.e. the purity of inner and outer life and says that "purity is something praiseworthy in whichever language it may be expressed and its opposite, impurity (kadar) is to be eschewed."[11]

In support of it he cites a tradition which explains the meaning of Ṣūfīsm and affords proof for it:[12]

"Abu Ḥujaifā told us that once the Holy Prophet Muḥammad visited us and his face showed us that he was deeply perturbed. He said : "The Ṣafw (pure part i. e. the best) of this world is gone and only its Kadar (impurity) remains." Consequently death is now a boon for every Muslim."

Imām Ghazzāli, under the heading—"On the way of the Ṣūfīs" in his book entitled Al-Munqidh min-al-Dalāl (Rescuer from Error) states:

"When after acquiring proficiency in these Sciences, I turned my attention to the methods of the Ṣūfīs, I came to know that their method attains perfection by means of theory and practice. The gist of their knowledge is to mortify the self and acquire freedom from baser passions and evil attributes so that the heart may get rid of the thought of any thing save God and to embellish it with Divine remembrance."

During the hey-day of his fame and glory, Imām Ghazzāli gave up his literary pursuits, and the job of Qādī. Adopting the ways of Ṣūfīs he wandered alone in forests. During this period, in one of his rambles, somebody met him and asked for a decision on some problem. He said to him, 'Avaunt ! You have reminded me of the false times, had you approached me when I was engaged in literary pursuits and was a Qādī, I would have issued a decree in the matter'. The eminent Imām now considered the lessons of the schools as humbug and he took that period for false times or a time of destruction. True it is—

O heart, thy high-prized learning of the schools,
Geometry and metaphysic rules
Yea, all but lore of God is devil's lore:
Fear God and leave this lore to fools.[13-14]

In praise of Ṣūfism Abu'l Hasan Nūrī says: "Ṣūfism is the renunciation of all selfish pleasures."[15-16] In other words it is giving up of unlawful carnal pleasures. A Ṣūfī is usually free from greed and lust and knows that "So long as he is a victim of lust he is, as it were, in a prison." He makes his self subservient to God's will, thus, his greed and lusts are annihilated. He is well aware that following the dictates of desires and lusts is misleading—is destructive. As the Qur'ān says:[17]

"And follow not the lusts (of thy heart), for they will mislead thee from the Path of God."

What a good advice was offered by Ba-yazīd Busṭām in these words:

Listen to a good word of the Sage of Busṭām
Spurn the lure of the grain if thou
carest not to fall in the net.[18]

To Abū 'Ali Qazwīnī "Ṣūfism is good manners".[19-20] Abū Sahl Sa' lūkī defines it as "Abstaining from objections".[21-22] Abu Muḥammad al-Jurayrī states : "Ṣūfism is the building up of good habits and the keeping of the heart from all evil desires and passions."[23] To Muhammad bin al Qassāb "Ṣūfism is good manners which are manifested by a better man in better times before a better nation."[24-25] Muḥammad b. Ali has expressed the view that—"Ṣūfism is goodness of disposition, he that has the better disposition is the better Ṣūfī."[26-27]

It is clear, then, that according to these great Ṣūfīs, Ṣūfīsm is nothing but the purification of the senses and the will. It is the effacement of one's desires in the will of God. It is the building up of a solid wall between the pure self and the Gog and Magog of passions and desires. It is, in a word, self-discipline—the avoidance of what is forbidden and the performance of what is ordained. Alkalābādhi thus sums up their "doctrine of the duties imposed by God on adults" : The Ṣūfīs "are agreed that all the ordinances imposed by God on His servants in His Holy Book and all the duties laid down by the Prophet (in the Traditions) are a necessary obligation and a binding imposition for adults of mature intelligence; that they may not be abandoned or forsaken in any way by the man, whether he be a veracious believer (Ṣiddīq), or a saint or a gnostic, even though he may have attained the furthest rank, the highest degree, the noblest station, or the most exalted stage. They hold that there is no station in which a man may dispense with the prescriptions of the religious law, by holding permissible what God has prohibited, or making illegal what God has declared legal, or legal what God has pronounced illegal, or omitting to perform any religious duty without due excuse or reason, which excuse or reason is defined by the agreed judgment of all Muslims and approved by the prescriptions of the religious law. The more inwardly pure a man is, the higher his rank and the nobler his station, so much the more arduously he labours with sincerer performance and a greater fear of God."[28]

In this sense Ṣūfīsm is a purely Islamic discipline which builds up the character and inner life of the Muslims by imposing certain ordinances and duties, obligations and impositions which may not be abandoned in any way by any man. The Prophet Muḥammad was sent to "instruct" mankind "in Scripture and Wisdom and to sanctify them."[29] The Ṣūfīs keep these "instructions" before their eyes, strive their utmost to perform what has been prescribed for them and to discharge what they have been called upon to do. God says, "And those who fight strenuously for us We will surely guide them into Our way"[30] and again : "Oh ye who believe ! Do your duty to God, seek the means of approach unto Him and strive with might and remain in His cause : that ye may prosper."[31] Believing in these exhortations the great Ṣūfī Yaḥya has said: "the spirit of gnosis will never reach thy heart, so long as there is a duty owing to God which thou hast not discharged !"[32] Thus Ṣūfīsm, in the words of Abū' Alī al-Rūdhbārī, is "giving one's lust the taste of tyranny" and "journeying in the pathway of the Holy Prophet."

Now I shall consider the definitions of Ṣūfism which lay stress on the building up of the inner life. What is meant by inner life itself would be made clear later.

Junayd ḥas defined a Ṣūfī as "dead to his self and alive in God."[33-34] He passes away from what belongs to himself and persists through what belongs to God. When he is dead in relation to his own self, he becomes alive in his relation to the self of God.

Ḥusayn b. Manṣūr al Ḥallāj thinks that a Ṣūfī is "Singular in his being, he neither accepts anybody nor does anybody accept him."[35-36] He feels the immediate Presence of God alone within and senses the Presence of God without and his mental faculty gets rid of the thought of anything save God and is totally captivated by God:[37]

> The eye does not see anything except God !
> Predication of everything is of Him only.[38]

When 'Amr b. 'Uthmān-Makkī was asked the meaning of Ṣūfism he replied:[39]

"A Sūfī is alive to the value of time and is given every moment to what that moment demands."[40]

O votary of earthly idols fane,
Why let those veils of flesh enwrap thy brain?[41]
'Tis folly to pursue a host of loves;
A single heart can but one love contain ![42] (Jāmī)

When Abū Muḥammad Ruwaym was asked to define Ṣūfism he said:[43] "Ṣūfism is nothing else save submitting one's own self to the will of God.[44] A Ṣūfī becomes dead to his own will and God Almighty's will alone functions in him and as a consequence of it, he has no wish of his own, neither does he want, desire or yearn for anything. In the words of Shaykh Jīlanī he now becomes:[45]

"At rest in body, contented in mind, broad-chested, his face beaming with the light of God, with an enlightened heart and oblivious of all things due to his nearness with God."[46]

Ma'rūf Karkhī defines Ṣūfism as:[47] "The grasping of realities and disregard of what is in the hands of People."[48] When the truth is revealed to the Ṣūfī that really God Almighty alone can inflict pain and bestow blessing, He alone can resuscitate and deal death to us, He alone is the Creator, the Cherisher, he becomes blind to every other thing except Him. In calamity and in affluence, he considers God Almighty alone to be the real agent, the real doer, and does not accept any other being as cause or instrument.

Shiblī says:[49]

"A Ṣūfī is severed from the world (Khalq) and connected with God (Ḥaqq) alone, as God Almighty had said to Moses, "I have chosen thee for Myself (for service)"[50-51] and have disconnected thee from others. Later addressing Moses He said : "By no means canst thou see Me."[52]

The same meaning is conveyed by what Dhu'l-Nūn said:[53] "Ṣūfīs are those who preferred God Almighty to all things and liked Him, God Almighty, too, then, preferred them to all things and liked them."[54]

The end and aim of a Ṣūfī's life is God alone; he loves God alone; his thinking, meditation and prayer are to God alone. He is ever ignorant of everything save God and when he thinks of God alone his mind is purified, and in this sense he finds himself attached to God and disconnected with everything save God. He is totally captivated by God alone!

Oh ! my soul's union with this fleshly frame,
Of life and death thou art the end and aim.
I pass away : thou only dost endure
When I say "me", it is "thee" I mean to name.[55-56]

If you think over the above definitions of Ṣūfism you will concede that its teachings are limited not to the purification of the will and senses, but confer on us nearness to God also as a consequence of which a Ṣūfi being lost to his sense of self-subsistence loses himself in the self-subsistence of God. He feels the immediate Presence of God within (Yāft) and senses the Presence of God without (shuhūd). His knowledge and actions are guided by God alone.

Now, I think it necessary to explain in some detail this summary statement.

The first step of a Ṣūfī is to teach a traveller on the path how to get released from the clutches of desires or lusts (hawā), how to emerge out of his own individual sphere of knowledge and enter into the knowledge of God. This part of the Ṣūfī's teaching is the same which is imparted by the Sharīat. Its gist could be expressed in two words : God alone is our Deity (Ilāh) i. e. He alone is our Master, Our Lord and our Helper. We worship God alone and Him alone we ask for help in all our wants and desires : "Thee (alone) we worship;[57] Thee (alone) we ask for help."[58] From the view-point of worship and help we are cut off from every thing save God and we express our humility and subjection before Him alone. This conviction is the Supremacy and Lordship of God Almighty purifies a man of all the baser attributes and embellishes him with all the nobler qualities; his heart is freed from unbelief, false worship, hypocrisy, innovation and sins and is filled with faith, unification, truth and virtues. To begin with, Ṣūfism means this sanctification of heart only. The same has been spoken of in the preceding definitions by eminent Ṣūfīs as "Purity of Character," "building up good habits and the purification of heart from all evil desires and passions." It has been also described as "good manners." Further elucidation of this point you will read in the first Chapter of this book.

When the Islamic faith imparts to us the knowledge that God alone is our Deity, Him alone we should worship and Him alone we should ask for help, the question then necessarily arises in our mind, 'Where should we seek this God whom we worship and before whom we express our humility and subjection ?' Truly speaking Ṣūfism gives a reply to the above question in the light of the Qur'ān and the Prophet's traditions, and it is also called "the Knowledge of the Nearness of God." ('Ilm-i-qurb). Really Ṣūfism is nothing but this knowledge only. The Ṣūfī who is conversant with the Knowledge of Nearness knows the secret of the relation between Haqq and Khalq, God and the phenomenal things, the secret of nearness and proximity, immanence and transcendence, Firstness and Lastness, Outwardness and Inwardness of God with the phenomenal things. Not only does he know this secret but he feels the immediate Presence of God within his own self. Now he is dead to his self and consequently we can call him the one whom God has drawn near to Him (Muqarrab). Note in Sūra LVI (WAQ'IA) in the Qur'ān, men are sorted out into three classes:

1. The Companions of the Right Hand (Aṣḥāb-al-Maimanā).
2. The Companions of the Left Hand (Aṣḥāb-al-Mash' amā).
3. Those nearest to God (Muqarrabūn).

The Companions of the Right-Hand are "those who believe in the Unseen", are "steadfast in prayer" and "have assurance of the Hereafter" in their hearts. The Companions of the Left-Hand are "those who reject Faith" and go after false gods. The Qur'ān describes them as "those who bartered guidance for error" and "have lost their true direction." This classification is, thus, according to the knowledge out of which spring their actions—knowledge of the right path and knowledge of the wrong path. But who are the "Muqarrabūn"? They are not just the Companions of the Right-Hand only, otherwise they would not have been placed in a different category. The Ṣūfis believe that it is just another name for those who are not only on the right path guided by their Lord, but also know the right relation between 'Ḥaqq' and 'Khalq' or between the Creator and the Created, between God and man.

To be more explicit, those who regard their Creator as their "Ilāh" or Deity and worship Him alone and ask for his help alone and believe that there is none other than He worthy of our devotion and able to help us, are called in the Qur'ān the Companions of the Right-Hand. And those who regard some created beings as their deities and worship them and seek their aid, thus rejecting the faith which lays down that God alone is our Cherisher and Sustainer, are termed the Companions of the Left. The 'Muqarrabūn' are those who not only believe their Creator as their only Deity and worship Him alone and seek for His help alone, but also know the true relation that exists between them and their Creator. They have been promised "Rest and Peace and a Garden of Bliss."[59]

Thus the great Ṣūfī Saint Shaykh Shahābuddin Suhrawardī in his famous Ṣūfī Compendium 'Awarif-al Ma'ārif (Chapter One) holds that though the term Ṣūfī is not used in the Holy Qur'ān, the word "Muqarrab" connotes the same meaning which is expressed by the term Ṣūfī.

A little later, once again he makes explicit: "Know that by the word Ṣūfīs we imply "Muqarrabūn" only, those whom God draws nearer to Himself."[60]

Now, you have read a very brief account of the knowledge of those 'nearest to God' (Muqarrabūn); you will read its details in the third Chapter of this book. This knowledge is concerned with the "Secret of the Omnipresence of God." The Qur'ān and the traditions definitely prove that the 'essences' of created beings are the 'other' of God. The relation between the Creator and the Created, is not one of 'identity but is definitely that of "Otherness", things created are the 'other' of their Creator. "Then will ye fear other than God."[61-62] "Is there a Creator other than God."[63-64] In spite of this 'otherness', the omnipresence, proximity, immanence, Firstness and Lastness, Outwardness or Inwardness of God, (or in the terminology of Ṣūfīs "identity") too, is indisputably posited by the Qur'ān and the Traditions. Apparently this would seem rather contradictory. We will have to consider it in the light of the Qur'ān and the Traditions and remove the contradiction. Ṣūfism

(The mystical knowledge of the Nearness of God or 'Ilm-i-qurb) removes this contradiction and proves—proves by the words of God Almighty—proves by the commentary of His Prophet—that the essences of phenomenal things before their creation, subsist in the Divine Knowledge, are the objects of God's Knowledge, are the ideas of God and are definitely the 'other' of their Knower, the Creator. For the 'essences' of things form, determination, limitation, individualisation are necessary. God is free from these limitations or determinations—is not a form. Being or existence does not belong to us. It belongs to God alone. We possess attributes of non-existence, and God Almighty is gifted with the superlative attributes of existence. Having no existence and existential attributes we possess no activity of our own. God alone is active, the only agent or doer.

In spite of all that is said above it is possible to posit in us what belongs to God, e. g. Being, Anniyya[65] (Self-consciousness) attributes, actions etc. How, then, these aspects of God Almighty were related to the essences of created beings and how was limitation caused in them ? Because it is quite clear that all these aspects are certainly found in us with the only difference that these are perfect, absolute and eternal for God and imperfect, limited and contingent for us. The explanation and the answers to these important questions in the light of the Qur'ān and the Traditions form the subject-matter of Ṣūfism and you will find an exhaustive discussion of these topics in this book.

Knowing all this the Ṣūfī (or Muqarrab) becomes aware of his 'poverty' (faqr). He begins to realise that kingdom and power, actions and attributes and existence really belong to God Almighty alone and that according to all these aspects he is a 'pauper'—a 'supplicant' ! (Faqīr). "O, mankind ! ye are the supplicants in your relation to Allah ! He is the All Sufficient, the Owner of Praise."[66-67] Therefore, he now sees that God alone is the Living, outwardly and inwardly: "The Living and the Self-subsisting Eternal."[68-69] He alone is the Knower and the Powerful outwardly and inwardly. "It is He alone who has Knowledge and Power."[70-71] He alone is the Hearer and the Seer outwardly and inwardly. "He alone is the One who heareth and seeth."[72-73]

By this distinction of his "poverty" he automatically gains the distinction of "trust" (Amānat); he begins to see that Huwiyya (Ipseity) Anniya (l-ness) and attributes and actions are found in him as a 'trust'. Therefore, the Ṣūfī exists through the Existence of God alone, lives through His life alone and knows through His Knowledge alone. Through His will and power he has power and will, hears through His hearing alone, sees through His sight and speaks through His speech. The Tradition of the Proximity of Supererogation (Qurb--i-Nawāfil) is aptly applicable to him in which is explained—

"My servant continually seeks to win my favour by works of supererogation until I love him; and when I love him, I am to him an ear and an eye and a hand. Through me he hears and through me he sees and through me he takes"[74-75] and according to some traditions:[76]

"I am to him a heart and a tongue, through me he understands and through me he speaks."[77]

Thus it may be said that God becomes the hands, feet, and ears of a Ṣūfī and probably the same meaning is expressed by Junayd when he said "God causes you to be dead to yourself and makes you alive in Himself." Then alone he will be able to say:[78]

"I bear only the name for its own sake,
the rest is He alone"

He has no life of his own, nor any being, but only as he lives in Him and He, by His Spirit, lives in him. Because God is, he is, without Him, he feels, he can do nothing and is nothing, not even a memory! Now realising his innate nature and being confirmed in the knowledge of his "poverty" (faqr) the Ṣūfī regards all created beings as dead and thus "Total disregard of what is in the hands of the people"[79] is created in his mind. He regards God Almighty alone as the doer and submits himself to the will of God. (Vide Ruwaym's definition of Ṣūfism above).

You will find an explanation of all these statements of mine and their vindication by the Qur'ān and the Traditions in the following Chapters. As Junayd has aptly remarked about Ṣūfism: "Our system of doctrine is firmly bound up with the dogmas of Faith, the Qur'ān and the Traditions"[80] and that which is refuted by the Qur'ān and the traditions is nothing but heresy !

There are two causes of heresy being mixed up with Ṣūfism:
(1) Peripateticism and (2) Neo-platonism.

After going through Aristotle and the works of other Greek philosophers the later authors crammed Greek logic and philosophy in the orthodox Scholasticism (kalām) and instead of refuting those objections and doubts raised against Islamic doctrines by the opponents, themselves began to examine theological doctrines and busied themselves in judging them by the standard of theoretical reasoning. Difference of opinions is sure to arise among the devotees of 'pure reason', that is why the history of philosophy is replete with contradictions and inconsistencies. Since the very beginning there were two parties among the Scholastics of Islam viz. the Ash'arites and the Mu'tazilites. The earlier Ash'arites made their reasoning subservient to divine knowledge and during their times those dogmas alone were accepted which were supported by the Qur'ān and the Traditions. Greek philosophy and logic did not influence them. But they laid special emphasis on the fact that the Mu'tazilites should be refuted, so that the common people may not fall a prey to their wiles. The Mu'tazilites (who are one of the groups of the followers of Wāsil Bin 'Atā, and excepting the question of Imāmate, the Shī'ites, too, in most of the tenets, agree with the Mu'tazilites) made their doctrines totally subservient to theoretical reasoning. The result was "that thrown into the wide sea and utter freedom of Greek thought, their ideas expanded to the bursting-point and more even than a German metaphysician, they lost touch of the ground of ordinary life, with its reasonable probabilities, and were swinging loose on a wild hunt after ultimate truth, wielding as their weapons definitions and syllogism."[81]

As regards the problem of the relation between the Creator and the Created, the Mu'tazilites denied the Omnipresence of God with the Created beings, because pure reason led them to believe that if the omnipresence of God be admitted with the Created beings, then by the divisibility of the created being it would necessarily follow that the Being of the Creator, too, is divisible. Further it would mean that God's Being is capable of incarnation and identification and this is clearly denying the transcendence of God. That is the reason why they interpreted in their own way all the Qur'ānic verses in which encompassment, omnipresence, proximity and immanence are clearly described. By doing so they thought that encompassment etc. should be encompassment etc. in knowledge only. The late Ash'arites too, with a view to making God's transcendence safe, made use of this sort of interpretation. But the truth is that in the Qur'ān we find verses of transcendence and verses of immanence in abundance. To believe in one and reject the other is the way of those who deny God and His apostles, as indicated by the Qur'ān.[82] The great Ṣūfīs have diverted our attention towards this fact. In this book you will find the true creed of transcendence and immanence and unless the right creed is adopted the true understanding of the Qur'ān and the traditions is impossible.

(2) When Neo-platonism found its way in to Ṣūfism its first consequence was that the "otherness" (Gairiāt) of objects was denied. The 'otherness' of the created things is clearly emphasized in the Qur'ān. Under the influence of the teaching of Plotinus phenomenal things were regarded not as other than God but identical with Him. God alone is, and other than God, in essence as well as in existence, is merely non-existent! "Everything is He" (Hamā ost)! The necessary outcome of the negation of the 'essences' of things and 'otherness of things' was heresy and ibāḥat (i.e. regarding everything as perm issible). There was now no furethrneed of following the Sharī'at (The Law), the antithesis of the Law and the Path (Tarīqat) was presented for the first time and thus a campaign was launched to throw off the yoke of the Islamic code. Islamic code was regarded as the creed of the imperfect, it was considered unnecessary for the Perfect to follow it; even the very conception of any other being save God was impossible. Sharī'at is compulsory so far as one has to admit 'otherness' when 'otherness' has been got rid of and God alone remained, there is no need to follow Sharī'at. "To follow beauty is the work of women and to follow majesty that of men." The Science of Sharī'at is "book knowledge" ('Ilm-i-Safīna) but the Science of Tarīqat is "heart knowledge" ('Ilm-i-Ṣina) which is bequeathed from

one mind to another since aeons, it is an arcane secret—a veiled mystery. Further details of these wild rhapsodies and a satisfactory refutation of them are given in Chapter IV of this book.

Another consequence of Neo-platonism was that the thing which was not the sole object began to be regarded as such and the real object was totally overlooked. Now higher achievements which are merely the necessary effects and are born by themselves began to be regarded as the sole object : ecstasy and 'states', 'Clairvoyant illuminations' and 'Control' (taṣarrūf), 'miraculous powers' and 'true dreams' etc. were considered to be the sole end or aim of a Sālik (the Traveller on the Path), and they were regarded as a characteristic symbol of holiness and piety. For the attainment of these feats unwarranted exercises and practices came in vogue, to learn and to be initiated in such sciences even the yogis and sanyāsis were not spared. Thus a hotch-potch of Indian rites, Greek theories and ideas took its birth and was known as Islamic Mysticism or Ṣūfism. The object underlying it was to possess extraordinary psychic powers and remarkable feats. The desire of attaining this super-natural power originated in the mind merely to show off one's superiority among people and to captivate their hearts. But real Ṣūfism, as you have read in the foregoing paragraphs, consists in steering clear of lusts and sinful desires and in realizing the Immediate Presence of God! It teaches us to be dead to self and attain everlasting life in God. How on earth could it have any relation with the so called Islamic Mysticism !

Here is the candle extinguished and[83]
there the living lamp of the Sun!
Do mark the difference between the
one and the other! (Ḥāfiz)

There is a vivid and lucid description of real Islamic Mysticism in this book, the object of which is the attainment of "abdiat" and the upshot of which is the realization of the Immediate Presence of God. The source of this Ṣūfism is the Holy Qur'ān and the Traditions of the Holy prophet Muḥammad. Probably for the first time it is presented to you with such lucidity and logical sequence. Some of the important points of the chapters of this book were orally explained to me by the perfect mystic, my master, Maulānā Muḥammad Husayn. Every line of this book is supported by the Qur'ān and the Traditions; it has also the support of the great Muslim Saints, though I did not deem it necessary to give references of their works. It would benefit the righteous person alone who has been blessed with true insight into religion, who has made his reasoning subservient to God Almighty's knowledge and who regards the Qur'ān and the Traditions the only criterion of right and wrong:[84]

He who understands what I say, has no
flaw in his insight.
No one can understand me except the one
who is gifted with insight?

CHAPTER II

WORSHIP ('IBĀDAT) IN ISLAM

O Thou—The object of my heart's craving ![1]
The force that moveth the madness of my brains !
Wherever I glance in this wide world,
Thee alone do I find each today and each tomorrow !

(Abū Sa'īd)

The first law governing the lives of human beings as well as animals is the acquisition of gain and the removal of pain. Preservation of self and reproduction of species are indispensable for both, so that man may seek things that help him in preserving and maintaining his life, and he may steer clear of things that would annihilate him or would lay his vitality. The fundamental distribution of things is based on this only. Things are either beneficial or harmful, useful or deleterious, good or bad ! When an organism is affected by them, sensations of pleasure, love, adoration and obedience are experienced; or feelings of grief, hatred and worry are excited. Out of these one is usually delectable and gratifying, the other is naturally odious and detestable; man strives to acquire one and avoid the other. The whole structure of human life consists of emotions—excited by those things, emotions—which overpower him and overthrow him; neither can he get rid of them nor can he free himself from their clutches until the prescribed course of his life comes to an end and he departs from this world saying:

I found the garden of this world just a cage,[2]
The birds therein only wavering desires,
From the morn to the eve of existence,
It all seemed to me but a fleeting moment !

During his short stay in this world every person keenly observes the metamorphosis of things. An eternal change is going on in the universe, nothing is permanent, nothing stands. One moment it is, another moment it is not. The caravan of existence never seems to be at rest, the glory of existence seems to be revivified every moment. Divine fury is annihilating everything every minute and Divine mercy is restoring life every second! As Jāmī has put it beautifully:[3]

"Being that disdains to be the same every second instant,
Assumes fresh splendour every fresh instant.
Look! "Every moment it puts on fresh glory"
If thou needest proof from the Book of God!"

When a person gifted with a keenly observant mind comes to know of the cause of this change and mutation, transitoriness and changeableness of things, the relation of dependence, which he had established with them owing to his need, want and penury, is abruptly severed; the penury of all the creatures is suddenly revealed to him and he now starts in quest of the Supreme Being who is exempt from chance and decay, who is Self-Existent and Self-Conceived, Who is a Necessary Being, an '*ens perfectissimum*', who possesses all the perfect attributes, has supreme powers, is the Master, Lord and Creator of the whole universe!

Now the gist of religion or faith amounts to this only that the relation of Dependence and Debasement[4] (which in religious terminology) is spoken of as the worship of one God[5] and seeking His help in all the affairs of life,[6] should not be established with finite beings and for fulfilment of one's desires or in want and need, assistance should not be sought from finite creatures; on the other hand, God Almighty alone should form the object of worship and source of assistance. The same idea is conveyed by the sacred article of faith—"There is none worthy of worship except God and Muḥammad is his Prophet"[7] who is sent to deliver this message to the whole world.

Want and penury are inherent in man's nature and to remove these he makes use of every beneficial and harmful object as his instrument, it matters little to him whether this object is one of the many elements of nature or belongs to the mineral or vegetable or the animal kingdoms. To fulfil his needs he takes help even from super-human and super-natural agencies and for help or assistance debases himself before them all. Owing to his ignorance and indiscretion he considers them to be "independently" beneficial and harmful and this alone forces him to bow his head in submission even to a creature that is far inferior to him.

To remove this deception of senses and delusion of intellect, the Prophet Muḥammad of Arabia delivered this message of Islam to the world that a human being, by virtue of the fact that he is the sublimest of all the creatures and the *chef-d'-oeuvre* of nature cannot humble himself by bowing before a creature lower than and inferior to himself. He should bow his head in submission before the all-benevolent, all-knowing, all-seeing and all-powerful Being alone whose mighty hands hold the reins of the whole universe—who possesses all the sublimest attributes and is exempt from all blemishes and defects. This Being only is our real Helper, this alone is worthy of our worship, to this only should we appeal for guidance, aid and assistance; this alone is our Creator, our Master, our God, our Sovereign Ruler. We are his creatures, mamelukes, slaves and subjects. Him alone we worship and to him alone we supplicate for the fulfilment of our needs and desires. He alone is opulent and we all are paupers who beg for his help, being his almsmen we are wealthier than all the plutocrats of the whole universe!

This message is nothing but gospel truth, it is absolutely in conformity with our self-respect. It is a correct exposition of the correlation between God and his created beings. The man who admits it is really a man in the true sense of the word. The object of the hopes and desires of this fearless and intrepid crusader is the only one God who is the master and sovereign of the whole universe. Now every action and movement of the crusader in his life becomes subservient to the commandments of this sovereign ruler and when in obedience to His orders he sacrifices one life, he is bestowed thousand lives in return. His weakness is replaced by strength, dishonour by honour, and indigence by riches. He does not fear any power on the face of the earth. The commandment in the verse of the Qur'ān "If you are a true Muslim, fear me only but do not fear them"[9-10] makes him fearless of all the world, neither has he any hopes of gain from anyone else. The verse "Does not God suffice for his creatures"[11-12] makes him unmindful of the whole universe. As soon as the ties of hope and despair are severed from finite beings, he acquires inner contentment and is reconciled with his Creator. Having pleased God he does not care for any being except God; now he is rich in every way. Is there anything greater than God which he might aspire to acquire? Most certainly not, he is now in possession of everything worth possessing. To that effect it has been said:[13]

"You may not despair over matters that pass you by, nor exult over favours bestowed upon you."[14] The man spoken of above only is the person to whom the words: "You alone are exalted, God is with you"[15] have been addressed.

Just see what a change the meaning of the term "Ilah" (One worthy of worship) has wrought within him. Before understanding the term he used to shrink and quake with fear like a humble and mean beast on confronting anybody, would take everybody for a harmful and beneficial creature, would bow his head in submission to him, would seek aid and assistance from him, passed the days of his life in their 'worship' only and got worried and perplexed! Not only he himself was frail and weak but the object he sought was also frail and weak.[17-18]

Now after gaining insight into the teachings of the Prophet and adopting its principles he takes the sword of "Lā ilaha" in his hand and steps forward. In the words of the Qur'ān he asks his ignorant comrades:[19]

"Is it some one other than God that ye order me to worship, O, ye ignorant ones."[20]

He is no more a slave and worshipper of a being other than God. For the first time in his life he experiences independence. The heavy load of fear is lifted off his breast. He bows low before his Creator and finds Him benevolent. The glad tidings conveyed in "He is full of mercy to the believers"[21-22] completely solace and comfort him. He now feels convinced that after faith in God Almighty, He would be benevolent to him. The fact that God being full of mercy is a wise and sovereign ruler, further fortifies his mind. He knows that God is the real 'doer' and finds every act of God full of the highest wisdom. According to God's commandments he entrusts every affair of his to him. "Take Him for thy disposer of affairs"[23-24] is the command of God. So after saying "Enough is God as a disposer of affairs"[25] he calmly and freely busies himself in his work. What a difference between this person and the one who believed that a being other than God has the power of conferring honour and dishonour! It is certainly true:

"The blind and the seeing are not alike, nor are the depths of Darkness and the Light, nor are the (chilly) shade and the (genial) heat of the sun; nor are alike those that are living and those that are dead."[26]

The substance or religion is that God alone is worthy of worship and He alone is the one whose assistance should be sought and its gist is preservation of the Tawḥīd. Now some details of this substance are mentioned below:

"Ibādat" (worship) : is a term for extreme 'servility or devotion' which is expressed before our real Creator, the notable methods of which are: prayers, fasting, alms-giving and pilgrimage to Mecca.

Prayers (Ṣalāt) : Just think over all the movements performed in prayers and the meaning of worship expressing your humility will dawn clearly on you. The devotee is thinking of saying his prayers; he is advancing towards the prayer-mat: on his lips are the words "I am stepping towards my Creator: he will guide me."[27-28] In his mind there is no idea of any being other than God. He considers everybody save God the Almighty beneath his notice. With this idea he gives utterance to the words "God is great"[29-30] and when in the presence of God he says:[31]

"For me I have set my face firmly and truly towards Him who created the heavens and the earth and never shall I give partners to God",[32] his whole attention is turned towards God ! Now he is devout and sincere in his mind. He is saying his prayers for God alone—saying it with the object that his faith might rise to the highest standard of perfection and not plod on as a routine matter. He is offering his prayers under the strong guidance of God the Almighty. In "Thanā"[33] he is expressing the omnipotence and greatness of God the Almighty and is admitting His unity by the words : "There is no one worthy of worship except Thee!"[34-35] Now with his hands folded, eyes bent downwards, he is standing in His presence the very picture of humility and modesty! With his lips he is repeating "Praise be to God"[36-37] and in his heart he believes there is no other being in the universe save God who merits our praise and that He alone possesses all virtues and beauties. When he says "The Cherisher and Sustainer of the worlds"[38-39] he is aware that the appellation "There is no Cherisher and Sustainer save thee[40-41]" could only be applied to Him. The whole universe is His. While saying "Most Gracious, most Merciful"[42-43] he feels optimistic, inspired with the feeling of God's mercy and grace. He realizes that God is Gracious to every creature of the universe, but mercy is a special characteristic reserved for the true believers: "He is full of mercy to the believers."[44-45] When he gives utterance to "Ruler of the day of judgment,"[46-47] he experiences the feelings of anguish! Doomsday is a stern reality—it is a day about which God Almighty has said: "It will be the Day when no soul shall have power to do aught for another."[48-49] In this state of hope and fear he says "Thee do We worship"[50-51] we express our humility before Thee, "And Thine aid we seek"[52-53] ignoring every being save Thee we turn to Thee whole-heartedly! Why should we address others for aid or assistance when we have been told and after experimenting have verified that nobody save Thee has power and strength! Others can neither harm us nor benefit us. After this laudation and admission of humility and bondage he implores and prays to God Almighty "Show us the straight way[54-55] 'the way of those on whom[56] Thou hast bestowed Thy Grace, not of those whose portion is wrath, nor of those who stray,[57] so that he might steer clear of temptations, come in closer contact with Him, and feel able to follow the foot-steps of true believers namely those of Prophets and Saints who alone deserve reward. He does not desire to follow those who were doomed to perdition and who, after turning to others than God for assistance and succour resigned themselves to eternal loss!

Together with this laudation and prayer he recites some more verses from the Qur'ān with a view to growing conversant with God's commandments, and impressing them on his mind by repetition. Suddenly, he bows in God's presence to express his deep reverence. In this manner he further expresses his servility, in the same state his lips give utterance to his Lord's eulogy and praise, and in his heart he has a vivid feeling of his own humility, meakness and helplessness. When he lifts up his head, God Almighty speaks through him "God listens to the praise offered to Him."[58] The head that bows before the Creator cannot bow before his creatures—this head is the most exalted of all, is pre-eminent and a priceless jewel. In fact, Almighty God polishes the person with His divine effulgence and makes him an invaluable jewel who approaches him. In gratitude for this boon the person eulogizes Him and falls down as it were, at His feet, catches hold of them and in this way expresses his humblest servility, his lips continue to give expression to his Lord's majesty, sublimity and grandeur. By such demonstration he experiences the greatest bliss. As the Prophet said: "The greatest bliss of my life is latent in prayers."[59] He is experiencing this bliss by observing his beloved Lord; this is the highest consummation of his desires—the ultimate goal which he devoutly wished for !

Infinite goodness alone is not a necessary attribute of the Creator. He should also be omnipotent, having complete power over all. By dint of infinite power and incessant might, He preserves us, fulfils our needs and desires. After putting our faith in Him, we become fully convinced that He would assist us and grant us victory. Being at a loss to explain the problem of evil, the Pragmatists denied the omnipotence of God but how could that God be considered a real Creator who is not Omnipotent at the same time? How can He help us who Himself cannot overcome evil? How can He be our Lord and grant us victory? It would be out of place here to discuss the problem of evil, but we admit that our Creator is omnipotent and possesses absolute powers. We consider him to be the real source of all actions and deeds. He alone is the source of power and might, consequently we seek assistance from Him and are confident of His being "The Best to protect and the Best to help."[61-60] As the Qur'ān ordains: "And hold fast to God ! He is your Protector—the Best to protect and the Best to help !"[62-63]

When He alone possesses power (as the Qur'ān says: "There is no power but with God"[64-65]) then He too is the fountain-head of all motion: "There is no power and no motion but with God." This is a truth applicable to God Almighty alone—a truth denied totally to His creatures. As soon as one grasps this truth, the veil of ignorance is lifted and he understands what the words "Not a particle of dust even moves without the command of the Almighty" mean. He no longer asks assistance of a being other than God and cries out "I bow (my will) to the Lord and Cherisher of the Universe!"[70-71]

As regards the methods of seeking assistance from the Creator, the Prophet has advised a number of them, out of which a few are given below:

Du'ā: Pray to Almighty God for the fulfilment of your needs and desires, it is one of God's commandments and Almighty God promises Himself: "Ask Me and it shall be granted unto ye."[72] There is not an iota of stinginess in Him, and nobody should despair and feel despondent after asking for what he desires. To comfort us God says: "Never give up hope of God's soothing mercy."[73-74] He is All-wise too, every act of His is replete with benevolence, He knows more than us what is good for us. If any of our prayers does not find favour with Him, it is due to the fact that rejecting it is good for us. In view of the above it has been said it is a test for a man to take rejection as a great boon. Some poet has, under the same impulse, translated the idea in the following lines:

"If disappointment for me is what pleaseth Thee,
Then believe me, I shall no more wish for any success!"[75]

Haḍḥrat 'Umar (May God be pleased with him) used to say, "I do not care for the state in which I shall wake up in the morning ! Let it be pleasant or unpleasant, for I do not know which state would be better for myself." God Almighty, Himself here instructs us and explains to us a very delicate point:

"But it is possible that ye dislike a thing which is good for you and that ye love a thing which is bad for you. But God knoweth and ye know not."[76-77]

After grasping the meaning of this point a Sage has said, 'Let all that happen which He desires should happen, let that not happen which we wish should happen.' Shiblī defines a 'Sage' thus: "A Sage is he who considers the rejection of his request more than a boon." From this point begins the stage of 'Resignation' which is the highest rank that a seeker may attain. Madam Guyon has thus expressed the idea beautifully:

Be not angry, I resign,
Henceforth, all my will to Thine!
I consent that thou depart,
Though thine absence breaks my heart!
Go, then, and for ever too,
All is right that Thou wilt do!

However if God Almighty does not grant the prayer of any true believer of His, He safeguards his heart, turns his mind away from the object he sought, keeps him away from indulging in grumbling, murmuring and whining, gets him to the stage of resignation and he on his part saying "For each period is a Decree established"[78-79] reconciles himself to God. Another form of granting his prayers is that the person does not achieve the object he sought but God Almighty does not turn his prayer down, averts some calamity which was about to happen, though the person concerned is unaware of this substitution. There is yet one last alternative, namely if the person is not favoured with the object he prayed for in his world, it is stored for him in the next :

"On the Day of judgement man will see those good deeds written in his Record which he will not be able to understand. He will be told that these are a sort of compensation for the object he prayed for in the world but was not destined to acquire it there."[80]

Any way the promise of God that a prayer is accepted is a true one; but this promise is absolute, it is not conditional or binding in the sense that it would be fulfilled at the same time and unconditionally as desired by the person. If you grasp this point you will come to know why the Prophet of Islam taught us to pray thus:

"Sufficient art Thou unto me, O My Lord, as You please, in whatever way You please and whenever You please and from where You please!"[81]

Trust (Tawwakal): Another way of seeking assistance is to entrust all of our affairs to the care of God Almighty. If we are convinced—not merely aware—that is, have a firm conviction, or to put it in modern psychological phraseology, if this thing is deeply impressed on our sub-conscious mind that the real agent or doer is God Almighty and that He Himself is the source of power and might and that He is merciful and benevolent to us when we believe in Him, then, we shall be glad to entrust all our affairs to Him ! After doing this all our cares and worries leave us, our hearts overflow with pleasure and contentment and we ecstatically repeat these lines:

"My concerns have I all left to the
care of my Beloved!
The consequence—life or death I
shall welcome with equal zeal."[82]

Trust in God is another word for becoming free from one's might and power, it is "holding fast to God."[83-84] Dhul-Nūn of Egypt has defined Trust thus:

"Trust is giving up of one's own devices and expedients, it is a stepping out of the sphere of one's own might and power." Sarī b. Mughallis Saqatī too agrees with him. The source of these definitions is the tradition of the Prophet Muhammad: "There is no power and no motion but with God"[85] and the saying of Lord God "There is no power but with God."[86-87] Trust is a mental process, that is, a person should be fully convinced in his heart that neither he nor anything else has either efficacy, power or motion; God Almighty alone has gifted him and everything else with attributes, power and motion. As He is my Creator so also is He the originator of my acts, He is creating my acts just in accordance with my essential nature. My essential nature is uncreated and unchangeable, being an 'idea' in the mind of God ! As God is uncreated, His knowledge or ideas are also uncreated. But the originator of my acts is God Almighty, consequently I have been given powers to exercise and use means, material as well as mental. I am employing these under orders. I am aware that if I desire to have an offspring I cannot give up coition; to satisfy my hunger it is imperative to take a mouthful in my hand, masticate it well and push it down into the gullet.

Trust here is not another term for deadlock and relinquishment of work; it is a term for knowledge and mental state, it describes a mental condition. It is a term for the firm belief that God Almighty Himself has bestowed power, motion and action on human beings. These powers have come into play since it was His will and pleasure that they should do so; if He wills the morsel of food cannot find its way in the mouth, the hand may be palsied and the food itself may be wrested from the hand. Our eyes are directed towards His action—they are fixed on His grace and mercy, we do not think of our manual strength nor of achievement. Our hands are engaged in work and our minds turned towards our Friend. "Trust is not the relinquishment of causes. It is the overlooking of the causes."

Having understood the rudiments, think a little over the question of 'Sustenance'! God Almighty has taken the responsibility of providing sustenance to every creature. Says the Qur'ān "There is no moving creature on earth but its sustenance depends on God."[88-89] Not only has He accepted the responsibility but also has sworn and has further cited an example :

"And in heaven is your sustenance as (also) that which you are promised. Then, by the Lord of heaven and earth this is the very truth as much as the fact that ye can speak intelligently to each other."[90-91]

God Almighty even provides for those who ignore Him and indulge in sins and those who are immersed head over ears in vices and gross offences; how then can they be deprived of their sustenance who obey his commandments? Generally he who plants a tree waters it; He alone succours the creatures who is their Creator. It is enough for the creatures that their Creator meets all their needs ! He himself is the inventor and succours us perpetually as well; He caused creation and the responsibility of feeding us lies on Him. An illustration of the above fact one finds in his own person. When a person invites somebody to dinner at his house, he makes arrangements to feed him sumptuously, when God Almighty has, by His will created us, He has consequently accepted the responsibility of feeding us; from His sumptuous table only we get our share of provisions. He is our Lord, our Master, we are His servants. As it is imperative for a slave to serve his master faithfully, so also it is now incumbent on the master to be benignant to his slave. If we become His devotees, if we do not worship anyone else save Him, and if we do not request anyone else for the fulfilment of our desires and needs, is it possible that He will not acquit

Himself of His responsibility? He is conveying to us these glad tidings in the following verse in the Qur'ān:

"And those who fear God, He (even) prepares a way out, and He provides for him from (sources) he never could imagine. And if anyone puts his trust in God, sufficient is (God) for him."[92-93]

The promise of God regarding sustenance is certain, we have only to discharge our debt of obedience and prayers to Him. If we do so it is impossible that He should invite us to His house and deny us His favours, grant us existence and leave us helpless, bring us into being and deprive us of His mercy, demand His due (worship) from us and do not favour us with our due. He is supremely benevolent, nobody will be a loser if he deals with Him and serves Him faithfully. "Is there anyone who asked a favour of Thee and Thou turned down his request, or wanted to make peace with Thee and Thou turned him out, came rushing towards Thee and Thou asked him to get out?" (Shaykh Jīlī). A lover has expressed the same idea in these words—'You think that you cannot subsist without food but food cannot be had without you'. Rūmī has admonished us thus:

"Why hanker after the means of Sustenance?[94]
Be patient, it will by itself come to thee one day!"

Rūmī again expresses the idea thus:

"Live in trust, do not stir your limbs,[95]
Thy sustenance careth for thee more
than what thou careth for it."

In any case according to the teachings of our Prophet we should endeavour to earn cur livelihood. But we must remember that our quest is not a constant or definite cause for securing our means of subsistence. Shāh 'Abdul Ḥaq of Delhi, commentator of traditions and the author of Futūḥ-al-gaib has briefly explained this point thus: "True, you get a thing only if you strive for it, but you don't get it by striving alone."[96] The same idea is conveyed by the following lines of a poet:

"No one achieves his object of desire
by simply striving for it,
Whoever achieves his object does so
by striving alone."[97]

The meaning of these lines is that we should not consider that striving is the definite cause of achieving our desire, as the whole affair is dependent on God's grace and mercy. Any way we should certainly strive, it is one of the Almighty's ways that He helps those who help themselves.

Patience (Ṣabr) : A third method of seeking assistance from God is to bear calamities patiently. The world is a place where sorrows and troubles abound, it is a prison, the warehouse of Beelzebub where nothing save evil and wickedness are found ! As the poet says:

Fie upon this world and its days ![98]
It is created to breed sorrow !
Its sorrows never abate for a moment,
For the king as well for the man in
the street !

"Man is born unto trouble as the sparks fly upward" says the Bible. A pauper and a king, a wealthy person or a beggar, all of them are beset with sorrows and pain and are victims of calamities. Says God the Almighty "We have created man into toil and struggle."[99-100] As God tests our powers of endurance, gets us in troubles,[101] tickles us to laughter,[102] makes us wail, destroys us and resuscitates us, and enriches and gives us satisfaction,[103] so he shows us, too, the way of warding off disasters. The remedy is patience.[104] How wisely He advises us :

"Oh ye who believe! Persevere in patience and constancy;[105] vie in such perseverance; strengthen each other; and fear God that ye may prosper."[106]

If in obedience to the Almighty God's commandments, we cultivate the habit of patience we shall be able to bear our troubles easily. If man will try to get rid of grief and misery by removing their cause, hoping thereby to live a life of ease, he will be disillusioned and sorely disappointed. Maulānā Rūm has beautifully expressed this idea thus:

"If you dart out anywhere in search of rest,[107]
Even from there trouble will befall you !
No place of refuge but it has its snares and
beasts of prey,
True rest you find in the Bosom of God alone !

If one is a true devotee of the Almighty and considers Him to be the Creator of all events, then certainly a calamity could be borne patiently and easily. The following example will clearly illustrate the idea: Suppose you are in a dark room, something hits you and you smart under the pain; you do not know who dealt that blow to you. When you send for a lamp and in its light see that he is your 'Shayhk', your father or any relation or beloved person from whom you never expected any injury, then the knowledge of this fact will undoubtedly console and comfort you, since in this painful state too you will observe the loving-kindness of the person who dealt that blow! Similarly in the line "But for thy Lord's (Cause) be patient and constant."[108-109] God Almighty is advising His Seeker to bear calmly and patiently whatever comes in his way!

If you are firmly convinced that God Almighty is Benevolent and All-merciful and are sure that He is ever kind and gracious to you, then you will take every pain and distress inflicted on you for a latent blessing. You should grasp this point well by means of illustrations! A loving father applies leeches to one of the limbs of his son's body but he does not intend to inflict pain on him. He is letting out the impure blood from his system which is acting as a toxin. A mother cannot bear to see her little son untidy. She rubs his body and gives him a wash with soap and warm water. The child cries, feels pain, but the mother does not intend to give him pain. Your well-meaning physician prescribes a medicine for you, and you dislike it but if he were to give you a medicine of your own liking you would never recover from your illness. If you are not given a thing on which you dote and you are fully aware that it is not being given to you out of consideration for your own supreme good, you will say that the act of not giving it to you is itself a great boon. Shaykh Abul Ḥasan Shādhlī has aptly remarked: "Know well, if God Almighty does not bestow anything on you, you should consider that this act of His is a great gift. But it is the truthful person only who takes the denial of a gift that way." The same secret has been hinted at in the verse: "It may be that ye dislike a thing, and God brings about through it a great deal of good."[110-111] That is the reason why the Prophet of Islam offered thanks on the infliction of disasters as he offered them on the bestowal of boons.[112]

We should have implicit faith and utmost devotion! Whenever a true believer is confronted with some distress he feels an aura of the presence of the Almighty in which he finds such pleasure that he bears the severity of the agony easily and he often does not feel the pain too, due to the predominating influence of His presence. If you are unable to grasp the meaning of the above lines consider the case of the lovely ladies who taunted Zulaikhā. Being enamoured of Joseph's bewitching beauty they incised the fingers of their hands by knives and did not feel pain! "When they saw him they did extol him and cut their hands."[113-114] This is also illustrated by the following insight of the Gnostics:

"By proximity to a beloved being the perception of pain vanishes into thin air."

After attaining perfection in faith and devotion you will perceive such secrets of mercy and blessing in sickness, distress and starvation that you will exclaim that the prophet of Islam spoke the truth when he said "Paradise is enveloped in all those things which the mind dislikes and hell is surrounded by carnal desires and sensuality."[115] "Self" is overpowered by calamities and distress, it becomes petty and humble, turns towards God Almighty, establishes a contact with Him and sever its relations with all others and is dead to the world! There is nothing more effective for character forming than grief; all the blemishes of the mind are cured by grief, the heart is purified and the soul is polished. If you succeed in treating your cardiac diseases by means of grief and distress and attain to the state of patience or perseverance, grief has aided you in achieving the greatest victory and such a grief is better than a thousand joys—the joys on account of which you were a slave to sensuality and licentiousness were enveloped in darkness and were far from light. You had no contact with the Almighty, the Evil one was your compeer, he had complete hold over you and you merited these words:

"If anyone withdraws himself from the remembrance of (God) Most Gracious, we appoint for him an evil one, to be an intimate companion to him."[116-117]

After acquiring knowledge of this philosophy of pain Ḥaḍrat 'Umar had declared "I found superlative luxury in patience" ! When Ḥaḍrat Abū Bakr Ṣiddīq fell ill people inquired after his health and asked whether they might send for a physician. He replied the physician had examined him; they asked him what the physician said; he answered the physician told him that "He did what he pleased."[118] Ma'rūf Karkhi would often say, "that person is not a faithful slave who does not enjoy the lash of his master, his claims of being honest are false !" In the pockets of some of the Gnostics these words were found written "Now await in patience the command of thy Lord: for verily thou art in our eyes."[119-120] Whenever they were distressed they would glance at this writing and by considering that God Almighty is aware of their affliction and is witnessing it, would dance for joy ! In view of the above a few holy men of the past consoled themselves when in trouble by repeating the above verse! It would be especially comforting for a believer to remember what the Prophet has said in this connection:

"When God loves a person He involves him in tribulation; if he bears it with patience He makes him His elected one and if he reconciles himself to Him He exalts him to the highest rank."[121]

Now, think over a general psychological law. Man can put up somewhat easily with ordeals and tribulations when he expects that he would be granted a good compensation for them. For instance, I am posted in a far-off country, away from my native land, cut off from my wife and family; of course, it is very tragic for me. But I do not consider it tragic, for at the end of a month I get the remuneration for my services in the form of salary. This remuneration makes me forget my worries, acts as a salve for my wounds. Keeping this principle in view think over the promises and glad tidings which are announced in the Qur'ān to the person who is struggling with tribulation patiently. It seems that all the good attributes of this world and the other are comprised in patience.

According to Imām Aḥmad, patience has been referred to in the Qur'ān at ninety places ! We will here speak of a few glad tidings which occur in the Qur'ān in favour of a patient person. If he keeps them in view and ponders over them with full conviction he would exclaim loudly, "An affliction inflicted by a friend is a gift and it is a sin to wail after receiving it."

Patience endears us to God Almighty:

"God loves those who are firm and steadfast."[122-123] Those who cultivate the habit of patience are dear to God and when one is beloved of God nothing should make him grieve and nothing should daunt him. Again: "God is with those who patiently persevere"[124-125] and these words are not a mere consolation. How can man suffer indignity with whom God takes sides ? He cannot come to any harm. When the Lord is on his side his enemies are powerless. Patience alone makes one the leader and he is entrusted with the duty of guiding people. "And we appointed from among them, Leaders, giving guidance under our command, so long as they persevered with patience."[126-127] The patience of a patient person serves as a weapon of defence against the wiles and cunning of his foes !

"But if you are constant and do right, not the least harm will their cunning do to you."[128-129] It is certain he will overcome them ultimately. "So persevere patiently, for the end is for those who are righteous."[130-131] He is sure to achieve his end. The promise made by thy Lord to the Israelites, namely, the promise that He would get them rid of their foes and bestow on them kingdom and power, was fulfilled on account of patience alone. The patient have been promised unlimited compensation for their patience. "Those who patiently persevere will truly receive a reward without measure."[132-133] Sulaymān bin Qāsim has remarked that requital for every act of ours is known to us, but the reward for patience being unlimited is unknown and beyond our ken. For the patient persons God Almighty has summed up all His praise, guidance and blessings together; and all these have been heaped upon them only and on nobody else.

"Give glad tidings to those who patiently persevere, who say when afflicted with calamity : "To God we belong, and to Him is our return"—they are those on whom (descend) blessings from God, and Mercy, and they are the ones that receive guidance."[134-135]

If ephemeral and temporary pain is borne patiently—and such pain is not unbearable, for unbearable pain is never inflicted on anybody—just think how one is being recompensed for it! What things are being promised him ? and who is it who is promising? Through whose lips assurance is being given ? If your heart is enlightened with the effulgence of faith, if it is not encased in a cover and not overturned, if it possesses the sense of perception and intuits these facts, is it not true that pain is a priceless boon for it ? Will it not enjoy it ? Will it not crave for it and will it not in wild ecstasy give expression to sentiments expressed in the following lines:

The poison that He gives[136]
 me is nothing but sweet,
This arrow of His is not vouchsafed
 to all sundry !
My Bosom Friend never gives me a bad turn,
The bitter he meets out is sweet enough
 for me.

Now pay heed to the sense of the following tradition:

"Just as an affectionate father takes care of his child so also God Almighty takes care of his creatures through tribulation."[137] The same were the perceptions of the apostles and of the Prophet of Islam and by dint of them they sacrificed every worldly possession for the sake of God.

Etiquette demands that while practising patience there should be no murmurs and grumbling. We should not complain to anybody else save God Almighty of our distress. As Jacob said : "I only complain of my distraction and anguish to God."[138-139]

Better my malady is hidden from the ken[140]
 of my boastful physicians,
Who knows the right recipe may come from
 the Domain Unseen.

Just think over the matter, what does complaining to creatures imply? Only this much that we are complaining of our distress to non-merciful and non-benevolent beings ! Such persons will never experience the sweetness of obedience to God in their hearts and soul. The essence of patience lies in concealing tribulations. The treasure-trove of goodness can be obtained by concealing the sufferings, the person who revealed them had no patience. But if in pain and agony a cry escapes from the lips it would not be contradictory to patience, provided a complaint is not implied by it and merely relaxation of anguish is aimed at, as by moaning the attention is diverted from pain and some amelioration is felt. Consequently there is a commandment about the permissible type of wailing and weeping which tells us that it does not conflict with patience and according to the tradition of Imām Aḥmad the first mentioned type of wailing is definitely against patience.

To be persevering and patient while confronted with a disaster means that one should meekly abide by the Divine decree even though one might be naturally feeling pain and grief. One must needs suffer pain, for it is but human to do so. The perfect man, Muḥammad, the Prophet of Islam, on the demise of Ibrāhīm said, 'O, Ibrāhīm, thy departure from this world has made us sad'. Any way the pain should not be a mental one, that is such a sad incident should not be considered inopportune and one should reconcile himself to it. One should repeat the words:

"What the King doeth is a thing of beauty" [41]

and mentally he should say:

'The ruler of Universe knows the art of running the Universe.'[142]

Now under the commandment, making use of necessary causes is not only valid but imperative and human nature is such that man does not rest until he finds out a solution to his difficulties. If in the use of causes one overlooks them and pays attention to their very Source the causes become more effective. If this method of treatment is applied and all its ingredients are mastered and kept in view, one gradually attains Resignation which is the greatest bliss and a paradise on earth as it were.

Praise (Shukr): The fourth method of seeking assistance is by means of offering thanks to God Almighty for the blessings He has conferred on us.

In his life man comes across Joy as well as Sorrow, suffers pain and enjoys ease, and there is darkness as well as sunshine for him. Due to their dullness of vision the pessimists laid down that the very source of the world is evil and eventually become the votaries of the 'Pandiabolism' theory. By their own experience they have found this world the worst of all, they could not find here anything real save grief and sorrow. On the contrary the optimists termed this world as the best possible world. According to them grief and sorrow are created merely for the sake of variety, by contrariety they heighten to a great degree the sense of pleasure; they are not real but only hypothetical. But speaking truly, sorrow as well as joy are real in this world. To consider either of them as an illusion is to deceive one's own self? Every person is daily verifying the truth of this statement by experimenting himself; he finds neither blessing nor calamity permanent. He is passing through every phase of blessing, he can deny neither the feeling of joy nor the perception of sorrow. The presence of joy and sorrow amounts to feeling them, and here only the remark of Berkeley that "*esse ist percipi*" seems to be correct. In fact the 'names' of God Almighty are majestic (Jalālī) as well as beautiful (Jamālī) and all these are perpetually at work. Not even for a moment they are inactive and inert. Good and evil, joy and sorrow, blessing and tribulation are all real and are the outcome of the bright effulgence of these 'Names'.

It is inherent in man's nature that he desires to get rid of distress and longs for more blessings. The wise teachings of the Prophet Muḥammad have chalked out mental plans for both. Patience at the infliction of calamities and offering of thanks when favoured with blessings create a tremendous revolution in the human heart. On the one hand, they rid him of wailing, breast-beating, despair and pessimism, and on the other free him from pride, arrogance, conceit and self-importance. Getting rid of these natal and injurious impulses, he becomes the repertory of courage, power and action. His vital energies are not wasted. They are directed towards the right object and concentrated on one point produce marvellous effects. While suffering hardships care should be taken to this extent only that the will does not weaken and one does not get discouraged totally. One should encounter distress heroically. This quality could be achieved by patience and while one is endowed with blessings, it is likely that he may become oblivious of God Almighty, who is the origin and source of all bounties and benevolence and thus he may be estranged from this source and enveloped in darkness. This danger is averted by offering thanks, as thankfulness consists in attributing a blessing to God. It should not be ascribed to one's own self or to His creatures because God Almighty Himself is empowered to inflict weal or woe, He alone can make or mar one's fortune. Though outwardly it appears that His creatures are bestowing boon son others, yet an observant mind is well aware that these are merely tools and instruments. The distributor, bestower and doer is God Almighty Himself. When keeping this fact in view, man offers his thanks to God, He favours him with more blessings, it is a definite promise of Him which admits of no exceptions at all. Says God Almighty "If ye are grateful, I will add more (favours) unto you."[143-144] The granting of our prayers, bestowal of means of livelihood and affluence, and pardon for our sins depend entirely on His will and pleasure; but the meed which one gets for offering thanks, in the form of extra favours is not contingent but absolutely certain. In view of this Prophet Muhammad has remarked : "Whoever is blessed with God's favours should offer his sincerest thanks to Him."[145]

The most fluent speaker of Arabia and Mesopotamia—the Prophet of Islam—has expressed this stupendous truth (on which depends the duration of favours) in another psychological way :

"Blessing is, as it were, a wild beast, keep it under control by binding it with chains of thanks-offering."[146]

It is a universal and necessary law of Psychology that when a person is favoured with a blessing he feels overjoyed but in course of time as he becomes more and more familiar with it it loses its value and worth after a few days. It now lacks novelty; he does not feel any difference in his life by its presence and in spite of living a luxurious life he feels bored. But if it is lost or wrested from him he would then appreciate it. 'The value of a blessing is realised after it is lost' expresses this truth aptly. Besides, losing the sense of appreciation of a favour is synonymous with losing the favour or boon itself. If a boon does not afford me pleasure and I feel mortified instead, then this boon is not a blessing but a curse. After understanding these truths you will come to know how far thanks-giving is instrumental in adding to the favours. A blessing would last if it is appreciated. Lack of sense of appreciation would mean lack of the blessing itself. Consequently the sense of appreciation of a favour should be kept alive and this object could be achieved by offering thanks. Ḥasan of Baṣra used to speak of thanks-offering as 'Gainer'[147] and 'Preserver'[148] because it safeguards the present blessings and secures unknown ones. By thanks-giving a blessing is safeguarded agains tharm and loss and as the sense of perception is developed in the feeling of blessings a man begins to observe those little favours which hitherto had been hidden from his view. Hence we can say offering of thanks definitely adds to the blessings. 'The thankful person deserves extra favours' is a psychological truth. That is the reason why the Prophet whenever he experienced any joy would bow humbly before God, the Almighty, to express his thanks. How queer is the nature of man! He quickly forgets the favours received from the Almighty and ever moans and complains of adversities. An Arab poet has aptly commented on the above thus:

> O, you insensitive to the values of life![149]
> Surely your insensitiveness will recoil
> on you.
> How long and how far
> Will you continue to complain only of misha ps
> and remain forgetful of blessings received?

Let us repeat those blessings showered on us which we do not see! Consider the 'blessing of gain'[150] and then the 'blessing of safety'.[151] Both of them are innumerable; while taking the blessing of gain into account a man should survey his own height and stature, should think over his health and physique and think of those delicacies which he enjoys while eating and drinking and while gratifying his sensuous desires. Later, in connection with the 'blessing of safety', he should see that he is not a cripple, he is safe from a thousand and one diseases and is secure against the wiles of his foes and adversaries. A true believer can think of a blessing from yet another view-point; he is endowed with the "blessing of Success"[152] and the "blessing of chastity."[153] The "blessing of success" means that he is gifted with faith, sincerity and perseverance; by the "blessing of chastity" is implied that he is safeguarded against unbelief, false worship, hypocrisy, apostasy, innovation and wickedness. If he were to enumerate the details of all these blessings, bestow a little thought on his own talents and capabilities and see whether he justly merited them, he would involuntarily exclaim:

> Without thee, O Beloved, I cannot rest,[154]
> Thy goodness towards one I cannot reckon.
> *Though every hair of my body becomes a
> tongue,
> A thousandth part of the thanks due to thee
> I cannot tell ![155]

How true it is "But if ye count the favour'[156] of God, never will ye be able to number them."[157] Now, how can man thank God for the myriads of His favours. Consequently it has been said, by offering thanks one realises how humble and weak one is. With the offering of one thanks-giving another thanks-giving becomes imperative. It is God Almighty Himself who motivates us to offer Him our gratitude and hence this motivation itself is a great boon for which we are bound to thank Him, then again gratitude for this gratitude is called for and so on *ad infinitum* ! Therefore, the appreciation of the favours received from the Almighty is gratitude, acknowledging his favours too is gratitude, the prayer, after acquiring them, to abide by his decisions is gratitude and eulogizing God when favoured by Him is gratitude!

The other methods of seeking assistance from God Almighty are briefly as follows:

Repentance : Whenever we commit sins we should sincerely turn to God in repentance. He assists us by granting us pardon "He pardons him who turns to him with a penitent heart"[158-159] What a comforting and affectionate message it is ! Says God Almighty: "But, without doubt, I am (also) He that forgives again and again those who repent, believe and do right—who, in fine, are ready to receive true guidance."[160-161] Repentance and penitence purify the heart of wickedness and ultimately this penitent person becomes the beloved of God

Almighty. "For God loves those who turn to Him constantly."[162]

We have discussed above in detail that power and authority are primarily the attributes of God Almighty only. "There is no power but with God."[163]

The relation of our hope and fear is established with God Almighty alone and as soon as it is firmly established, He makes us oblivious of all His creatures. In consequence of this we are freed from the grip of that murderous emotion which deprives the lives of those who seek help from others beside God, and of peace and contentment for ever. This emotion is fear which keeps on biting, pulling about and destroying peace of mind! It is because of this we behold a net in every nook and a ferocious animal in every corner!

Remembrance (Dhikr): If we seek help from God Almighty in the matter of remembering us and desire that He should be pleased with us, we should 'remember' Him and abide by every act and decision of His. "Then do ye remember Me, I will remember you."[164-165]

Resignation (Riḍa): When once we are resigned to Him He is pleased with us. "God well-pleased with them, and they with God."[166] As a poet says:

> They who seek zealously the pleasure of God,[167]
> Most meekly tread the path of His Will,
> They do what God asks them do,
> God does what they wish Him do!

The gist of all that we have written above is that faith or religion consists of two parts—worshipping God alone and asking for His aid only. ('Ibādat & Iste'ānat). "There is none worthy of worship except God and Muhammad is His Prophet."[168] If we admit the truth of the above words with our lips and heart, the presence of any other deity save the one Almighty God vanishes into thin air! How sublime must be the heart which is freed from the conception of other being than God and in which the divinity of God Almighty has taken root! God Almighty alone is the object of his worship, desires and aspirations; He is his sole Master and Helper. His heart is illumined with the glory of the unity of God; it is enlightened with faith and is full of piety. Such a person is beloved of God Almighty who is his supporter, his trustee, his master, his preserver and his guide !

In this connection you should remember a few definitions. As you have already seen "Tawḥīd" consists in considering God alone as worthy of worship and God alone to be the one whose help can be sought—as Lord and Helper, and in sincerely believing Him to be so : If we admit and confess it, "Shrk" '(joining others in worship with God,)' makes its exit out of our hearts and "Tawḥīd" takes its place. By testifying to the prophethood of the holy being (Muḥammad) who gave us this message and by believing him as the true Prophet of Islam, 'Kufr' or infidelity leaves the heart and in its place 'faith'[170] reigns supreme. Two things are comprised in Faith as well as in 'Tawḥīd'. Faith includes the testimony of the prophethood of Muḥammad and the conviction that God alone is worthy of worship and God alone is the one whose assistance should be sought.

Hypocrisy (Nifāq): is mere verbal assent of the creed and its denial at heart. An 'Innovation'[171] too is a curse, it is equivalent to introduce a new idea in religion and to justify it as a principle of religion. To hold an un-Islamic code as valid and just in lam is an Isinjury to God Almighty and to some extent a claim to prophethood. An innovator rarely repents since he believes that 'innovaticn is praiseworthy, why should he then be repentant ? In view of the above Muḥammad, the Prophet, has remarked : "Every innovation is misguidance"[172] and misguidance leads to perdition !

Before embracing Islam it is imperative to repent of Unbelief[173] and request for the Almighty's pardon; then one should bear testimony in his heart to the fact that God alone is worthy of worship and Muḥammad is his Prophet. After that one should verbally admit the same fact. By doing that, the conception of a being other than God, deeply rooted in the mind, will be annihilated and the divinity of the Almighty God will take its place. Now one would steer clear of hypocrisy, apostasy, innovation and wickedness and persevere in living a pious life. This is 'religion' or 'obedience' about which Maulānā Rūm has aptly remarked:

Shouldst thou love liberty and care to[174]
develop a loving heart,
Bind thyself to Him in devotion now and
for ever.
Life is meant for devotion alone,
Life without devotion is a matter of shame!
Save humility, devotion and restless yearning,
Nothing is of value in the Sight of God.
He who lives in love,
To him all save devotion is infidelity.
Devotion to be fruitful must rest on the
inward urge,
The seed to grow into a plant needs a
kernel within!

Says God Almighty:

"O, Prophet, say thou : "This is my way :[175] I do invite unto God—on evidence clear as the seeing with one's eyes—I and whoever follows me. Glory to God ! and never will I join gods with God."[176]

CHAPTER III

TRANSCENDENCE AND IMMANENCE

There is naught in the Universe save[1]
One Light!
It appears in a variety of manifestations.
God is the Light; its manifestations, the
Universe
Unification is this, the rest is illusion
and tall talk.

"He is the First, and the Last, and the Outward and the Inward and He is Knower of all things."[2-3]

It is the teaching of Islamic Faith that God is our Deity, He alone is our Lord and Creator, Him alone we worship and from Him alone we seek assistance. But the question is, where should we seek this God, whom we worship and before whom we express our humility and subjection? We have been informed that He is our First, our Last, our Outward, our Inward, is close to us, is near to us, is immanent and is with us. Then what are we and who are we that God is to be known only through a knowledge of our own selves? Of what use to us is the store of formal sciences without this science of self? What useful purpose do they serve at all? As Rūmī says pertinently:[4]

Thou hast turned into a philosopher but
thou knowest not
Where thou art? From where thou hast come?
And what thou art?
O, ignoramus! when thou knowest not thyself,
Why, then dost thou pride thyself on thy so-called
knowledge?

But this knowledge of self, the Sūfīs assert, should not be acquired by resorting to happy guess-work or haphazard thinking. On the other hand, it ought to be gained according to the Qurān, as instructed by God, and according to the Traditions, as preached by Prophet Muḥammad. In the quest of the truths of faith the eye of reason has the same power which a born blind possesses in the perception of colours. Or to express the same idea in the words of Maḥmūd Shabistrī;[5]

The light of reason applied to the
very light of life,
Is as the eye of the head applied
to sun.

Were it possible for a person to become a Self-knowing and Truth-knowing gnostic by the study of Logic and the Sciences of dialectics and eristics, nobody would have doubted about the saintliness of Shaykh Abū Ali Sīnā and no one might have controverted the idea of Fakhruddīn Rāzī being a confidant of the deep truths of faith. Reason, probably, guides one as far as the portals of God Almighty's abode, but a step further towards Him depends entirely on His Grace and Mercy:[6]

Reason can but take you to His threshold,
It is only His grace which can lead one
to Presence!

A gnostic has expressed the same truths of faith aptly thus:[7]

If thou couldst but know thyself as thou
shouldst,
Thou wilt gain the knowledge of the Universe.
If thou shouldst care to know the Truth,
Know thyself, not through speculation,
But through illumination, search and faith
Be thou own knower, for this is the way to
know the Truth.

Now the guidance of the Qur'ān is sufficient to impart the knowledge of Self to us. Considering the 'Creation verse' (Āyati-Taqlīq) we find that the word 'Thing' is applied not only to all the objects of the Universe, but to our own 'self', too. Says God Almighty Himself about the creation of objects:[8] "Verily, when He intends a *thing*, His Command is "Be", and it is!"[9] It is evident that God is here addressing a thing; the Command, (the object of which is the thing) is 'Be'. Now there are two conjectures here—either the thing is 'existent' or is 'non-existent'. In the first instance, the Command 'Be', would be meaningless. There would be no sense in a thing coming into existence, which is already existing. If the thing is entirely non-existent, then, too, the Command would have no meaning. How could a thing be addressed which does not exist at all? Consequently, it is necessary that the thing which the Divine Will desires to bring into existence externally and which is the object of His address, should subsist in His mind and should be non-existent only externally. The following words of God denote the external non-existence of things:[10]

'I did indeed create thee before, when thou hadst been nothing.'[11]

These Qurānic verses prove two things:

1. Everything before creation is the object known to God. It subsists in the mind of God. It is imperative for the Creator to possess knowledge of his creatures prior to creating them. A further proof of this is afforded by the following verses:[12]

"Should He know not what He created; And He is the Subtle, the Aware."[13]

"He is the All-wise Creator."[14-15]

Even after creation it is known by God: "He is the Knower of every creation."[16-17]

The Qu'rān is making it explicit by the above verse. Therefore, in essence, everything is an "idea" of God, object 'known' by God; it subsists in the Divine Knowledge and is contained in His Being.

2. Everything is externally a creature, the Lord God is its Creator—"God is the Creator of everything."[18-19] The Qurān amply supports this statement. The essences of things before creation subsist in the Divine Knowledge, are the objects of God's knowledge, are the 'Ideas' of God and these alone are the objects of His Command and have an aptitude for emerging from the inward into the outward and when according to their urge make their appearance at the word of command, they are termed 'Creatures'. In view of the above, the whole world has been termed 'contingent', which means that it depends for its mental as well as external existence on something else. The world of things owes its mental existence to God, because things are the ideas of the Divine Self, and are existing externally, on account of Him, as they are gifted with external existence, by the Command of God Almighty alone, and in their existence they are thus absolutely dependent on Him. They

borrow their existence from Him; before creation they were void of external existence, were 'relative' not-being and the words:[20] "When thou hadst been nothing,"[21] aptly described them.

Now think over the nature of the relationship between the creator and creatures, the Knower and the known. This relation is not one of 'Identity' but is definitely that of "otherness." Between the Essence (Dhāt) of the Creator and the essences of His Creatures, the Essence of the Knower and the essences of the known, the relation of 'otherness' is clearly seen!

A painter conceives, say, the idea of a garden, he then paints it on the canvas. The garden exists as an idea in his mind; depends for its (mental) existence totally on his mind. The painter's mind is the 'Substratum' of the idea. The idea is a 'form' i.e. it has determination, is limited and confined. This cannot be said about the painter's mind. It is free from these determinations and limitations. The Knower and the Known, the mind and the mental image, are by no means identical. The painter is not the painting, neither the painting, the painter. They are totally different from one another.

Similarly, it could be said without comparison, that a relation of complete otherness is found between the Essence (Dhāt) of God and the essences of things between the Knower and the known, between the Creator and the Creatures.

Now, as was shown above, things are internally the ideas of God. God being a Knower from eternity knows His own thoughts—these being the objects of His knowledge. Now the Ṣūfīs call the ideas of God "al a'yān al thābitā," the Fixed Prototypes, or the Latent Realities, or merely the Essences of things, which when manifested or created are called "external objects" or "Created things", or, merely the many 'things' of the world (Khalq).

Let us now analyse more fully the internal aspect of things, things considered as the ideas of God or "Essences", i.e. before they are created externally. Even as ideas, things are not identical with the essence or Dhāt of God. Now what constitutes the difference between God, the Knower, and the ideas of God or essences which must now be termed as "the Known?"

This may be briefly expressed thus:

The Known	*The Knower*
1. Is a form possessing limitation or determination or individualisation.	1. Is free from any limitations or determination—is not a form.
2. Subsists in the mind of the Knower, does not possess its own independent existence. The Ṣūfīs call it "a relative non-existent."[22]	2. Exists in Himself, depending on nothing else but Himself.
3. Possesses no attributes, e.g., life, knowledge, will, etc. though possesses the capacity of acquiring those attributes, if given.	3. Possesses positive attributes e.g., life, knowledge, will, power, hearing, sight and speech. (These are called the primary attributes of God.).
4. Is passive, having no existence and existential attributes of its own; possesses no activity of its own.	4. Is active.

From the above statement it is clear that the relation between the Known and the Knower is one of 'otherness', never of 'Identity'. The essence of things are the ideas of God, co-eternal with God. God is 'one', His ideas are 'many'. God exists independently, ideas depend on the mind of God for their existence. The essence of God is free from any limitation or determination; the ideas, though unlimited in number, are limited or determined in form, possessing their own peculiarities or characteristics or essential nature, termed "S͟hāklāt"[23] in the Qur'ān.

If the ideas or essences are 'the other' of God, things which are just the external manifestation of ideas, must, for the same reason, be the other (or g͟hair) of God. God manifested externally what was contained in the essence or the essential nature of things. God transcends the limitations and determinations of things. Says the Qur'ān:[24] "He is not in the likeness of anything; He is the hearer and the seer." Again:[25] "Praise and glory be to Him: For He is above what they attribute to Him." The essence or Dhāt of God being absolute is free from all limitations and, as all things are necessarily determined, "God is not in the likeness of anything" and is "above what they attribute to him." How can God be identified with things? How can the Creator be the same as the Created? Essentially things are different from God, and this difference is not merely suppositional but is a real difference—difference of essences, the essence of God being the other of the essence of things. God is comparable to no created beings. He is transcendent in the sense of being a necessary being, self-begotten, self-caused, self-existent, independent and absolute in contradistinction to the contingent, created and determined beings of the phenomenal world. He is transcendent also in the sense that He is unknowable and incommunicable and beyond all proof, as the Qur'ān says:[26] "God keeps the knowledge of His Self hidden from you."

The relation between God, the one, the transcendent Being ("not in the likeness of anything") to the many things of the universe may be expressed in theological language thus:

The One	*The Many*
Khaliq (Creator)	Makhlūq (Created beings)
Rabb (Lord)	Marbūb (Slaves)
Ilāh (The worshipped)	Malūh (Worshippers)
Mālik (The Master)	Mumlūk (Servants)

Thus the gist of the whole doctrine so far stated is that man cannot become God, as some people considering Islamic mysticism to be a phase of Pantheism are led to suppose.

Muḥyid Din-Ibn al 'Arabi presents the same truth in his Futūḥāt when he says:[27] "The 'Abd has no limit set for 'Abdiyat that he might cross the limit and develop into Rabb. Even so the Rabb has no stations of His own beyond which He turns into an 'Abd. Hence Rabb remains Rabb without end and 'Abd' remains 'Abd without end.[28]"

The Shaykh has again expressed the same sense in the following beautiful couplet:[29]

The 'Abd will remain 'Abd whatever
the progress he might make.
The Lord will remain the Lord however
low He may descend.

And the author of Gulshan-i-RĀz says:[30]

Say not the contingent out-steps
its limits
Contingent becomes not necessary,
nor necessary contingent.
He who is transcendent in spiritual
mysteries
Says not this, for it is an inversion
of verities.*[31]

Ḥaḍrat Shāh Kamāluddin presents the general rule thus:[32]

Keep in mind the Ṣūfī's fundamentals
The Khalq should not become Ḥaqq,
Abd not become Rabb
O, thou insensible, it is not true
at all to call
Scent, wine; water, mirage; good, evil.
Posit a real duality between the Real
and the Phenomenal,
Else talk not of verities, keep your
mouth closed.

A gnostic has said: "Ḥaqq is Being and the 'Abd is Not-Being, and the transformation of essence is impossible, therefore, Ḥaqq is Ḥaqq and the 'Abd is 'Abd, That is to say:[33-34]

'Abd is 'abd and God is God and
that for ever,
God forbid ! The 'abd and the Ma'bud
are never the same !

From this total dissimilarity and otherness between the Knower and the Known, the Essence of the Creator and the essence of the created, and the Essence of the Lord and the essence of the 'abd, it is now clear that the essence of the Created or the Known is totally devoid of existence, attributes, Lordship (Rūbūbiat), Ownership (Mālikiat), and Rulership (Hākimiat). When we gain knowledge of this "want" this 'poverty' (faqr) of our being we understand this, too, that these aspects, being, existence and attributes etc. are peculiar to God alone, and because of these aspects His being only is free of all wants, worthy of all praise. The same meaning is conveyed by the verse.[35] "O, mankind ! ye are the supplicants in your relation to Allah. And Allah ! He is the all sufficient, the Owner of Praise."[36]

From the first part of the Article of Faith[37] "There is none worthy of worship except God, and Muḥammad is His Prophet" too, we gain the same knowledge. The infidels looked upon idols as their Deity and believed in their divinity, but for divinity it is imperative to admit Lordship (Rubūbiat), for if these idols were not considered the doer, the sustainer, the supporter, the helper and master, they would not have been worshipped, and the qualities of divinity would not have been attributed to them. Now for actions, attributes are indispensable, because they alone are responsible for actions; attributes are impossible without existence, existence alone is their source and origin. The word 'La' (none) negates divinity from idols, (i.e. the essences of contingent beings) negates Lordship and negates attributes and existence. The word "Illa' (save) affirms these aspects in the Being of God. Thus from "There is none worthy of worship",[38] too, we learn the 'want', 'poverty' (faqr) of the Essences of contingent beings and absolute Self-sufficiency of the Essence (Dhāt) and from this view point complete dissimilarity and otherness is found between the two.

I consider it necessary to state once again, the summary of whatever details I have given above, in the light of the Qurānic verses, though I do fear, it would be a repetition, yet the importance of the subject compels me to do so.

Uptil now the knowledge (which is necessary for acquiring the gnosis of God) we gained about our Dhāt or Essence is that our essences are 'ideas' subsisting in the mind of God, and are 'other' than the Dhāt or Essence of God. For ourselves, form, determination, limitation and individualisation are necessary. God Almighty is free and exempt from these limitations or determinations—is not a form. Being or existence does not belong to us. It belongs to God alone. We possess attributes of non-existence, and God Almighty is gifted with the superlative attributes of existence. We do not possess attributes of existence and God does not possess attributes of non-existence or not-being. Having no existence and existential attributes we possess no activity of our own. God alone is active—the only agent or doer.

In short, what is ours does not belong to God and what is God's does not, originally, belong to us. If we posit the attributes that belong to the Created beings in God, it would necessarily mean Blasphemy or Infidelity, [Kufr], and if we posit the attributes of God in the Created beings it would necessarily imply 'Shirk' or association of others with God as co-equals or-co-partners, and if we posit that God Almighty's things are meant for Him alone, we acquire Tawhīd (Unification).

In spite of all that was said above it is possible to posit in us what belongs to God, e.g. Being, Anniyya [I-ness] attributes, actions, etc. Now the question is, how these aspects of God were related to the created beings, and how was limitation caused in them? For we see, that all these aspects of God are found in us, the only difference being that for God these are perfect, absolute and eternal and for us imperfect, limited and contingent. In the rest of this thesis I shall try to give an exposition of these important questions and answer them.

The fact is that despite this total disparity and obvious otherness between the Dhāt or Essence of God and the essences of created beings, the omnipresence, nearness, immanence, 'firstness' and 'lastness', outwardness and inwardness of God are also asserted by the Qur'ān and the Traditions. Apparently this seems to be a strange thesis, combining two irreconcilables—transcendence and immanence! Let us solve this problem in the light of the Qur'ān and Traditions as Shabistrī says:[39]

> To him, whom God guides not into the road,
> It will not be disclosed by use of Logic.[40]

The Qur'ān asserts that God is immanent in all beings whatever. This immanence is indicated in various ways: God is with us:[41] "And He is with you wheresoever ye may be. And God sees well all that ye do."[42] The word "Wheresoever" [Aināmā] generalises place, and the phrase 'ye may be' [Kūntūm] generalises time and because of His time and personal omnipresence with knowledge, God said:[43] "He sees well all that ye do", i.e. whatever you do at any place or at any time is taken note of by Him. God sees all this Himself, consequently on other occasion He says:[44] "They seek to hide from men and seek not to hide from God. He is with them."[45]

Nothing could be hidden from God, since He is always with us. This verse clearly furnishes proof of God's presence with us. Remember well the word Allah[46] in 'Allaho Ma'nā'[47] and the pronoun 'huwa'[48] in Huwa Makūm[49] have been used in the same sense. In these there is no possibility of any other meaning save the literal one, consequently this verse definitely establishes His presence with us, and is indisputable!

Now take note of a Tradition, too. The Prophet Muḥammad said:[50]

"Anyone of you, while offering prayers, should not spit in front of himself, as God Almighty is before him." From this tradition Ḥafiẓ Ibn-i-Ḥajar Asqālānī has argued:[51] "This tradition refutes the idea of one who confines God to the 'Arsh (the Throne) only." Therefore the general omnipresence of the Supreme Being is clearly obvious.

Haḍrat Shāh Walīullah, has translated the verse, in Fat-ḥur-Raḥmān thus:[52] "He is with you wherever you may be" and in Qaul-al-Jamil he says about the contemplation "God is with me".[53] "Consider yourself to be quite close to God in spite of the fact that His Being transcends all space and direction."[54]

In reply to a question Haḍrat Shāh 'Abdul 'Azīz of Delhi, says:[55] The verses of the Qur'ān and the Traditions of the Prophet Muḥammad clearly establish the omnipresence and personal proximity of God. Is it just that we regard what the Law [Sharī'at] has laid down as invalid and call the imagination of our imperfect reason as legal and valid?"

(2) God is *near* us: Says the Qur'ān.[56] "And we are nearer unto Him than ye are, but ye see not."[57] Here the antecedent of the pronoun "We" [Nahnu] is Dhāt; by joining it with the conjunction "but" [Lākin] the possibility of the "attributive" nearness too is removed, since it is evident that attributes are secondary concepts and are conceived by reasons only. Personal nearness is something sensible and is perceived by sight. Here God Almighty did not say "ye know not"[58] or

"ye do not understand."[59] He said "ye see not"[60] as the Dhāt is not [like attributes] a merely secondary concept, within its personal limits it is given to us in sensation. Apart from this delicate point, presence in Knowledge together with His Dhāt or Essence is definitely proved in another way. God Almighty says:[61] "We know what his soul whispereth to him, and we are nearer to him than his jugular vein."[62] Here the word "and" has been placed between two sentences for the sake of clarification; it explains the persence in knowledge described in the first sentence from personal presence in the second sentence. The fact that for knowing 'whisperings' or 'thoughts' of the soul, personal presence or proximity is imperative, is proved by the 'occasion of revelation' of the following verse:[63] "And when My servants question thee concerning Me, then surely I am nigh."[64]

Ibn-ī-Ḥātīm referring to Mu'āwiyā bin Ja'ad says:[65] "Once a bedouin inquired of the Prophet Muḥammad whether the Lord God was near to him that he might have a tete-a-tete talk with Him, or was he very far which would necessitate to call Him aloud ?" After hearing him the Prophet maintained silence for a while. The following verse was then, revealed: "And when My servants question thee concerning Me, then surely I am nigh." This statement infallibly proves that by the nearness of God is meant 'personal nearness' and not the one gained through knowledge. How beautiful a poet expresses this idea :[66]

The slumber of ignorance has flung me off
  from the Presence of God !
Truly there is none so close to thee as
  thy Friend !

For a further proof of 'personal proximity' think over another tradition which runs as follows :[67]

Abū Musā Asha'arī said that once he accompanied the Prophet together with others on one of his journeys. His companions commenced to say "God is Great" very loudly. On hearing it, he said; 'O people, do not be too hard on your ownselves [i.e. say it gently]. You are not addressing any unseen or deaf Being, you are calling the Being who is listening to you, seeing you and who is with you. The One whom you are addressing, is nearer to you than the neck of your camel."[68] This tradition is an exposition of "We were never absent [at any time or place]"[69-70] and accounts for "Surely, I am nigh."[71-72]

Imām-i-Rabbānī, Mujlf-addid-i-Ai-Thāni explains the 'Nearness of God' thus:

"Though the nearness of God is definitely established by the Qur'ān, the fact is there that God is beyond the reach of human reason, understanding, knowledge and intuition. This transcendence works for nearness and not for aloofness. Indeed He is nearer than the sense of nearness. The truth is that we feel the very Being of God nearer than His attributes of which we are but mere reflections. This perception is beyond the reach of theoretical reasoning. For reason cannot conceive of anything which is nearer to us than reason itself. We failed to find an illustration to explain it. The only proof is the Qur'ān and genuine inspiration."[73]

The following couplets of a gnostic explain the verses of Qurān beautifully:[74]

> Read from the Book of Truth: "We are
> indeed close to thee"!
> Know well thy relationship with God!
> God is nearer to us than our own selves,
> Through ignorance we but wander from
> door to door in search of Him.

Shaykh 'Ali-al-Mahayemī, in his commentary of the Holy Qurān, viz., Tabṣīr-al-Qur'ān, expounds the verse:[75] "We are nearer to him" thus:[76] "His Presence is neither in terms of space nor time nor station. On the other hand He is there in His Essence without admixture, infusion and union."[77]

Haḍrat Khwājāh Bāqi-Billāh ascribes distance and remoteness to a superstition. Says he:[78] "When you come to know that this is the reality, you find that nearness and distance are a creation of our own imagination. There was no distance between you and God which necessitated an effort for coming near to Him, neither was there any separation which required an attempt for a union."[79]

(3) God encompasseth all things:[80] "Allah ever surroundeth all things."[81] Ah indeed ! it is He that doth encompass all things."[82-83] The word 'Allah' is a proper name and it signifies a Being who possesses all the attributes and not some one particular attribute, such as knowledge or will. The pronoun 'huwa' refers to the same Being, therefore, these two verses unquestionably prove that God surrounds and encompasses all things, and admit of no further explanation. A proof of this is furnished by Ḥadīth 'Dalaw' and other traditions.

While answering the queries of the Jews Haḍrat 'Ali had remarked:[84] "God is Glorious. He is Superior to the concept of one who asserts that our God is space-bound. He indeed knows not his Lord and Creator. He is Superior to the concept of him who says that space encompasseth Him. If only he would reflect over it, he is bound to feel bewildered and confused. Verily it is He who encompasseth every space."[85]

This statement of Haḍrat 'Alī supports the Qurānic proposition: 'God encompasseth all things'.

Imām Bayhaqī in his Kitāb-al-Asmā wa Ṣifāt quotes from Abū Da'wud thus:[86] "Sufyān Thawrī and Shūba and Hammād and Sharīk, and Abu 'Awānā never imposed limits on God, nor instituted comparisons about Him, nor likened Him to anything." The doctrine of these scholars of yore, that the Infinite Being could not be limited, is the proof that God surrounds all things. Imām Abū Hanifā[87] has condemned him as an 'infidel' who limits God in the upper direction and in the lower direction and Imām Shāfiyī says:[88] "Reason is prohibited to impose limits on God or to institute comparisons about Him."

It would be necessary here to clear a doubt. It has been asserted in the Qur'ān at one place:[89] "That Allah surroundeth all things in knowledge."[90] Those who deny that the very Essence of God encompasseth all things, argue that the encompassment spoken of in the verse:[91] "Allah ever encompasseth all things"[92] should also be encompassment in knowledge only. In one verse encompassment is spoken of as absolute and in another it is defined by knowledge. According to the rule of the doctrines of Fiqh, therefore, the encompassment of God should be understood as encompassment in knowledge only.

This doubt has been cleared by the Ṣūfīs by different ways, the gist of which is as follows:

1. In 'aqāyad' (dogmas) the principles of Fiqh are not authentic.

2. The doctrine of Fiqh which is being applied here is that of the Shāfiyī sect, the Ḥanafī sect opposes it. The Ḥanafī sect applies a general rule to a general statement and a particular rule to a particular statement. Consequently where the 'encompassment' is general or absolute that would be its meaning and where it is defined by knowledge that would be its sense.

3. If we even admit the Shāfiyī principle, then, too, it is obvious that the very Essence of God encompasseth all things, as the separation of an attribute from the Essence is impossible. Attribute and Essence are the necessary concomitants of one another. Therefore it follows that where there is encompassment in knowledge there the Essence is also present to encompass all that it knows.

(4) The Omnipresence of God: His ubiquity.

"And whithersoever ye turn, there is Allah's Countenance."[93-94] As God encompasseth all things so He is present in His Essence in everything. Wheresoever you turn your face, or whatever thing you find, the Divine Essence, too, will be found there, since nothing could exist without the omnipresence and companionship of God Almighty:[95]

He has neither quality nor quantity about Him
He is in every corner never disappearing.

Commenting on this verse Shāh Abdul 'Azīz says:[96] "Wherever you stand and turn your face towards Him and divert your attention towards Him, at the same place will you find His presence and his proximity."

In the verses:[97] "Everything will perish save His countenance"[98] and "Everyone that is thereon will pass away; there remaineth but the Countenance of thy Lord of Might and Glory."[99-100] Shāh Rafīuddin has explained the word "Countenance" as Dhāt or Essence. The import of the verse:[100] "And whithersoever ye turn, there is Allah's Countenance" has been tersely stated by Sha̲h Ismāīl S̲h̲ahīd, as "Present every-where."[102]

The Essence [Dhāt] of God and the Being of God are identical. In the first volume of his Maktūbāt, [Maktūb 234] Imām Rabbānī has furnished proof of this and summing up says:[103] "The Being of God is the same as the Essence [Dhāt] of God." Similarly Sha̲h 'Abd al-'Azīz of Delhi, maintains that Being is nothing else save God's Essence. In his S̲h̲arḥ Fiqh Akbar, Mulla 'Ali Qārī has remarked:[104] "Being of God is identical with the Essence of God." Therefore the meaning of Essence and Being of God is identical.

Note a few more verses in support of the fact that God Almighty is present in His Essence with everything. In the verse:[105] "Lo! Allah is Witness over all things"[106] we are being informed that God witnesses all things, as by "Shahīd" [according to the Persian Commentary of Hiṣn-i-Hasīn] is meant "One who is present and from whom anything which may be known or seen or heard cannot disppear."[107] As the word 'Allah' is a proper name, and 'witnessing' (S̲h̲ahādat) is its attribute, and as an attribute could never be separated from Essence, it follows necessarily that God essentially is present with everything.

The same meaning is conveyed by the verse:[108] "In whatever business thou mayest be, and whatever portion thou mayest be reciting from the Qur'ān—and whatever deed ye (mankind) may be doing we are witness thereof when ye are deeply—engrossed therin."[109] Since God is present with Created beings, so He witnesses every state, every action and every activity of theirs. The proof of this personal witnessing is further furnished by the words of Jesus Christ quoted by the Qur'ān by way of a fable:[110] "I spake unto them only that which Thou commandest me, (saying) : Worship Allah, my Lord and your Lord. I was a witness of them while I dwelt among them and when thou tookest me thou wast the watcher over them. Thou art witness over all things."[111] This assertion of Jesus Christ, viz. "Thou wast the watcher over them"[112] is deduced from God Almighty's statements.[113] "And God doth watch over all things[114] and "For God ever watches-over you,"[115-116] it is evident that knowledge, is impossible without personal presence, as attributes and essence are inseparable.

In this connection I will cite a last verse which will lucidly prove the Omnipresence of God:[117] "We shall show them Our potents on the horizons and within themselves until it will be manifest unto them that it is the Truth. Doth not thy Lord suffice, since He is witness over all things. How! Are they still in doubt about the meeting with their Lord? Lo! Is not He surrounding all things?"[118]

Here God Almighty has asserted that He is Present with everything in person, and then emphasised this Presence by His Divine encompassment, because the Being that encompasseth all things must necessarily be present with everything, and consequently would be visible. Those who have doubts about the meeting with (immediate vision of) their Lord, are not acquainted with the secret that He sorrounds and encompasses all things, hence they are doubtful!

(5) The 'firstness', the 'lastness', 'outwardness' and 'inwardness' of God.

"He is the First and the Last and the Outward and the Inward and He is the Knower of all things."[119-120] It is obvious that the pronoun, 'He' refers to Dhāt or the Essence of God, and all these four terms are definitive in character and purpose. For the prefix 'Alif Lam' is used always to signify definitiveness in concept. By it in all the four aspects of existence viz. the first, the last, the outward and the inward, God's Being alone is posited and the existence of any being other than God is negatived. Further, there is no fifth aspect where it could be posited.

Thou alone art the First and the Last,[121]
why wrangle over the question of
temporality and eternity?
Thou alone art the Outward and the Inward,
why, then, talk of Being and Not-Being?
The First that never changeth place;
the Last which never passeth away,
The Outward and the Inward both without
quality and quantity.

The Commentary of the above verse could be found in the prayer of the Prophet Muḥammad, which has been cited by

Abū Dāwūd, Muslim, Tirmidhi and Ibn-i-Mājā from 'Abu Hūreyrā:[122] "You are the First and there is nothing before You; and You are the Last and there is nothing after You. You are the Outward and there is nothing above You. You are the Inward and there is nothing below You."

The meaning of the first sentence is that God Almighty alone is the First and there is nothing before Him. By this negation it is not meant to negate the essences of things, which subsist in God's knowledge and whose 'otherness' is firmly established by irrefutable Qurānic verses, and is posited in this verse, too, by the words, "He is Knower of all things."[123] Only the existence or being of the things is negated. Negation of existence is evident from the following verse also:[124]

"I did indeed create thee before when thou hadst been nothing."[125]

This again is supported by the following Tradition.[126]

"God was and there was nothing before Him."[127] Thus the existence of things has been negated from eternity or the first aspect.

The meaning of the second sentence is that God alone is the Last and there is nothing after Him. Thus the existence of things has been negated from 'abad' or the last aspect.

The third sentence means that God alone is the Outward, there is nothing above Him, since existence has preference over the essences of things. The essences of things are relative not being and Existence is a further addition to them. For the same reason existence alone is manifest from every form of thing, The meaning of "Lo, Allah is Witness over all things"[128] is now clear, and the secret of "And whithersoever ye turn, there is Allah's Countenance"[129] unravelled. After discovering this latent truth we now understand the saying of some gnostics:[130] "I never behold anything ere I behold God Himself."

> Thy face is visible through this world,[131]
> who says Thou art hidden ?
> If Thou art hidden, how there comes in
> the world ?

The immediate vision of the Being of God in everything is due to the fact that God is the Outward or the Evident and there is nothing above Him. The following verse carries the same sense:[132]

"Is then He who standeth over every soul (and knoweth) all that it doeth, (like any others)?" God is 'standing' over or present in everything. The same conclusion could be drawn from:[133] "God ever encompasseth all things" and "God is witness over all things."[134]

When God alone is the First, and the Last and the Outward, then, He alone would be the Inward, too. That is the reason why the Prophet stated: 'You alone are the Inward, and there is nothing below You'. In this way from all the four aspects of existence the existence of 'things' has been negated and the existence of God alone posited. This is the correct commentary of the verse:[135] "He is the First and the Last, and the Outward and the Inward" which the Prophet of Islam has given. It would amount to unbelief (Kufr) if we refuse to believe what he has said, and to hypocrisy, if we doubt it, and 'innovation' if we add anything to what he has said, and to be faithful we will have to admit verbatim what has been said. So it is our firm conviction that:[136]

Thou art the Ever Before and Thou the
    Ever after too,
Thou art the Inward and Thou the Outward too,
In Thy attributes Thou art the Encompassing,
In Thy Being Thou art All-Sufficient and
    Transcendent.

"How can Love deny there is nothing in being except He."[137-138]

The verse, "He is the First and the Last,"[139] could be explained by yet another authentic tradition which is known as "Hadi<u>th</u> Dlaw". It proves the Immanence of God by many reasons. I think it necessary here to make mention of it. A part of this tradition is:[140] "If you let the rope descend to the lowest depth of the earth even there will it assuredly touch God," and then the prophet quoted from the Qur'ān: "He is the First and the Last and the Outward and the Inward and He is Knower of all things".

This is the last sentence of a prolix tradition, the gist of which consists in expressing two facts. The Prophet spoke to his companions about the magnitude of each sky and its distance from the earth and in the same way counted the Seven Skies and took them to the Divine Throne ('Arsh). There is another tradition known as Ḥadīth-i-Aw'āl, which has been cited by Tirmidhi and Abū Dāwūd from 'Abbās bin 'Abdul Muṭṭalib. There it is stated that the Prophet after counting up to Divine Throne asserted[141] "Then there is God above this". After giving the knowledge of what is above the Throne the information regarding the lower region was necessary. Now in Ḥadīth-i-Dlaw, he turned his attention from the higher to the lower regions i.e. from the First to the Last, and when after describing the distance of all the seven strata of the earth reached the lowest region, said that under the lowest region, too, is God. For the verification of the truth of both the statements, he recited the verse "He is the First and the Last" so that God's Omnipresence and Immanence may be proved in the Throne ('Arsh) as well as the sky and in the earth i.e. with all things.

In Ḥadīth-i-Dlaw and Ḥadīth-i-Aw'āl some facts are especially noteworthy.

In Ḥadīth-i-Aw'āl the Prophet stated that God is on the Throne and did not confirm his statement by an oath, because:[142] the fact that "The Beneficient One is established on the Throne"[143] is stated in the Qur'ān, hence oath was not necessary. On the other hand, he took an oath to prove God's Omnipresence and Immanence in connection with the lower earth, as he might have felt that the pervasion of a singular Being over the higher and lower regions and in everything, which is in them, could not be easily comprehended. Here doubt or denial was possible. That is why he confirmed his statement with an oath, so that there might be no room for an interpretation or comment and the persons addressed might be convinced. With this end in view he cited the verse: "He is the First and the Last", which is a clear proof of the Omnipresence of God. Thus according to the verse:[144] "He is Allah in the heavens and in the earth"[145] the same Being manifests Himself in heaven and earth, serenely in all His glory. Hence a mystic involuntarily exclaims:[146]

> On whatever we cast our glance, by God,
> Nothing we behold is aught but God !

The two worlds are He, all else is
illusion ![147]
My dear, do not involve yourself in
vain thoughts !

The summary of the above expositions is that 'Existence' belongs to God alone, and the concomitants of existence (attributes and actions), too, are peculiar to Him. God alone is the First and the Last, is the Inward and the Outward, is near and present and close and Immanent. But the question arises; Whose First and Last is God ? Whose Outward and Inward is He ? Whom does He encompass ? And with whom is He understood to be ! An answer too has been given above,[148] viz. all these relations are established with the essences of things only. If there subsist no 'essences' of things, neither the conceptions of Firstness and Lastness, nor those of Inwardness and Outwardness, Nearness and Proximity and Omnipresence and Immanence are possible. You have noted above[149] that these Essences are the ideas of God and by virtue of their being known, subsist in the Divine Knowledge, and are contained in His Being. They are the object of the divine Command, "Be", and have the aptitude of emerging from the inward to the outward. They are "other" than God. The Essence (Dhāt) of God being "not in the likeness of anything" is free from all the limitations or determinations of the 'essences' of things.

Now, the question is—and it is admittedly a poser—How are the essences of things, which are the ideas of God and are a species of accidents subsist in the knowledge of God, able to derive existence and attributes of existence ! What is the mystery contained in the Command "Be and it is" ! Is it possible to unravel the Secret of Creation !

Now, there can be only three logical possibilities about the coming into existence of the essences of things or ideas.

1. Ideas came into existence without any Substratum underlying them. This possibility is, in the light of reason, impossible, as ideas are accidents and the appearance and manifestation of accidents without substance is inconceivable. They subsist in the mind of God before creation, and they cannot make their appearance without any substance even after creation.

2. Ideas are the accidents of some Substance, but this Substance is other than God. This conjecture, too, is false, because we have seen above that God alone is the Real Being or Substance.

Beware ! Everything except God is perishable ![151]

3. Ideas are the accidents of some substance and this substance is the Absolute Being alone. This is as it were, their *materia prima* in which they subsist and on which they depend. The same sense is expressed by the following verse:[152] "He that created the heavens and the earth from Ḥaqq. High He be, exalted above all that they associate (with Him)"[153] as Exalted (taālā) is the adjective applied to Ḥaqq and the lexical term for the Necessary Being is Ḥaqq. The verse[154] "Then exalted be Allah the king, the Ḥaqq"[155] is referring to the same fact. At another place, God for the sake of definitiveness says:[156] "We created them not save from Ḥaqq".[157] At another place He is also addressing those who have knowledge thus:[158] "Allah created not (all) that save from Ḥaqq. He detaileth the revelations for people who have knowledge. '[159] On another occasion He is imparting knowledge to the true believers thus:[160] "God created the heavens and the earth from Ḥaqq. Verily in that is a sign for those who believe."[161] According to Shari'at and the lexical definition Ḥaqq alone is the word for the Absolute Being. Considering derivation the root of Ḥaqq (God) and Ḥaqiqat (reality) is one and the same. All the ideas, or the essences of things have appeared from Ḥaqq and are manifested in Ḥaqq. Therefore the Essence (Dhāt) of God and His very Existence is at work in the creation and origination of the world. This is the secret of "He is the Outward"[162] which is explained by the verse:[163] "God is the Manifest Truth"[164] i.e. God alone is manifest or God alone is 'Ḥaqq' who is manifest. The verse[165] "God is the Light of the heavens and the earth"[166] further supports this statement. The Essence (Dhāt) of God, which is nothing but Absolute Existence, by virtue of its manifestation is called "Light" (Nūr), as Light is that which is "visible in itself and which makes other things visible." This exactly is the attribute of God (Ḥaqq) who exists by Himself and makes other things visible. For the same reason the term "The Outward" has been applied to God—the Absolute Being. As the

essences of things, prior to creation, subsist in the knowledge of God as ideas, so also all things exist externally in this One Being and become visible by His attribute of Light. For your guidance and information I shall now disclose the arcane secret. May God grant you understanding to grasp its meaning:[167] "God guideth unto His Light whom He will."[168]

"God in His own Immutable state, Attribute and Being without altering His Individuality, manifests Himself through His Attribute of Light in the forms of phenomenal objects, which in reality are but reflected entities, expressing outwardly the essences which subsist in the Knowledge of God, and hence it is that the Divine Aspects (Being, attributes etc.) came to be associated with the world of creation or phenomena."

He is the First and the Last and the Outward and the Inward and He is Knower of all things."[169-170]

> The Same incomparable Being in His
> incomparability,[171]
> Has manifested Himself in the form
> of everything.
> Let me tell you the story plain of
> my friend,[172]
> Everything is from Him, and if you
> look aright, He is Everything !
> His charm shines from every particle
> in the Universe
> Only the layer upon layer of presumption
> came in as a veil between ('Irāqī).

Whatever I have just stated, though terse, is enough[173]— "None will grasp their meaning save the wise."[174]

Note well, that creation of things does not imply that they have been created out of pure Nothing, because out of nothing nothing comes; nor does it mean that the absolute not-being manifests itself in the form of things, as according to the definition itself, absolute not-being is not a thing at all which could become the matter of any being, or could be moulded into the form of a being. Further neither could God be divided into parts because He transcends all limitations and individualisations. God reveals or manifests Himself in the form of phenomenal objects and this revelation or manifestation takes place in accordance with those ideas or essences of things, which are latent in God (Ḥaqq) and subsist in His knowledge. It is as a result of this revelation or manifestation, phenomenal objects make their appearance in the external, according to their aptitudes or capacities. Every thought form, that is, the essence of thing or the created being, according to its aptitude and original capability, is being benefited by Existence and existential attributes.

Be clear in mind that being or existence of phenomenal objects (Khalq) can exist only in some one form or other of the manifestation of the Being of God Himself, and this manifestation cannot but assume the form of one or other of the phenomenal objects themselves. In the words of Shaykh Akbar, one reflects the other.[175]

"Hence God is thy mirror wherein you see your ownself, and thou art His mirror wherein He beholds His own Names and their working."

The eminent Jamī has expressed it in the following couplets :

Essences are mirrors wherein God
reflects Himself.
Or God's Being is the mirror wherein
essences reflect their forms.
In the eyes of the clear sighted
gnostic,
Each of the two mirrors is a mirror
to the other.[176]

In other words, phenomenal objects (Khalq) are manifest in the reflexive mirror of God's Being and God is manifest in the reflexive mirror of the phenomenal objects (Khalq).

Thy manifestation is through me and my
being through Thee,
Without me thou canst not manifest thyself,
and without Thee I could not have come
into being.[177]

The Being of God (Ḥaqq) and the essences of phenomenal objects (Khalq) are always inseparable as these essences are the ideas of God, and the knowledge of God is not possible without the ideas. He who separates the one from the other is necessarily ignorant. The following couplet of Shaykh Akbar is easy to understand:[178]

Were He not and were we not,
What has happened would not have happened!

i.e. Creation is dependent on the Being of God and the essences of things, both of them are interdependent, as God (Ḥaqq) is manifest in the form of things and things are existing on account of the real existence of God:[179] "Our existence is due to Him and His manifestation is duc to us."

The real secret and the mystery of Creation could only be clearly understood when, by His Grace and Mercy, God Almighty unravels the intrinsic nature of Tajalli (Manifestation). Through the agency of the heart of a 'Perfect man' about whom the following statement of Shaykh Akbar finds the aptest application:[180]

He who has contained God in him, how can
he feel narrow
For the world! What do you think of such
a person, O you, who hear me?

God Almighty has disclosed this secret to my humble self. Consequently, in obedience to the instruction of this 'Perfect man'[181] I am making you my confidant and probably this is a decent way of offering thanks to God Almighty for His favours. 'Beware! lest you lose your way and go astray.'

Tajalli or Self-manifestation or revelation is supported by the Qur'ān and Traditions. If you desire to discover its intrinsic nature, think over your ownself for a while. Suppose, you bring to your mind a picture of a dear friend of yours, who is strolling in his garden with his wife and children. As soon as you *think* of him, your mind assumes the form of your friend and presents itself before you. But in spite of this manifestation, notwithstanding the determination and limitation of the images in which it is appearing, and despite their multiplicity, your mind is one without being multiple, is free from all the limitations or determinations of these thought-forms.

After discovering the nature of self-revelation or manifestation (tajalli) in intuition, you will be able to understand easily how God Almighty, as He is, and maintaining His Immutability without change and multiplicity, without infusion (ḥulul) and unity (ittiḥad), without division, is manifesting Himself in His thought-forms through the attribute of light (Nūr). The manifold variety of ideas and their determinations (which is a proof of their being other than God) cannot make any difference in the personal Unity of God and His transcendence. The same sense has been conveyed by Shaykh Akbar in Futūḥāt by the words:[182] "God, the transcendent; God, the Immanent". The manifestation of God's transcendental Being in various forms is proved by the Qur'ān as well as the Prophet's Traditions.

The meaning of tajalli, as we have seen is manifestation or revelation and for this 'form' is imperative. The word tājallā appears in the Qur'ān in the following verse:[183]

"And when the Lord revealed (His) Glory (tajalla) to the mountain, He sent it crashing down. And Moses fell down senseless."[184]

It is clear that this self-revelation pertained to the same Absolute Being that Moses was unable to behold. At another place it appears that God Almighty is manifesting Himself before Moses on Mount Sinai through a tree or in the form of light and fire.

"But when he revealed it, he was called from the right side of the valley in the blessed-field, from the tree: O Moses! Lo! I, even I, am Allah, the Lord of the Worlds."[185]

During the Day of Judgement God Almighty will reveal Himself in some forms as the Qur'ān hints:[186] "The Day that the "Shin" be laid bare, and they shall be summoned to bow in adoration."

Now, turn your attention towards the Prophet's Traditions. In the tradition cited from Abū Sa'id Khidrī, which is known as the Tradition of Taḥavvul, it has been lucidly explained that during the Day of Judgement God Almighty will reveal Himself to every group in the form of their deities.[189]

"On the day of Judgement the announcer will ask loudly every group to follow whom they worshipped. All those who worshipped deities other than God, having a shape or not having any shape, such as stone, wood, etc. will find their way into Hell and worship their deities there. Now there will be left those pious persons and sinners who worshipped God Almighty alone. The Lord of the worlds will, then, come to them and say, "Whom ye are waiting for, whereas every group has followed its own deity ?" They will reply "O Lord, we had disassociated ourselves from these people in the world itself, though we needed more their help and support, in spite of it we did not keep their company (and according to Abū Hureyrā's reference to the tradition, they will say, "This is our ultimate goal, when our Lord will come to us, we will recognise Him"). God Almighty will ask them, "Have ye any token by which you can recognise Him ?" They will say, "Yes, we do have." Then God Almighty will make His appearance through "Sāq" or "Shin". The word "Sāq" is a comparative (tashbihī) attribute of God. The Absolute Divine Being can never manifest Himself without a form. Manifestation is always possible in forms, modes or determinations only. God Almighty who is the Inward preserving his Own Being, reveals Himself from absolute Inwardness (butūn) and occultation, (Istitār) in the forms of Phenomenal objects, according to his own Name, the 'Outward' ! The above tradition clearly furnishes proof of tajalli or self-revelation and manifestation and change of form. The same fact is supported by the traditions of Ṭibrānī and Ḥākim:[190] "The Lord will appear before them in assumed form."[191] As assumption of forms (tammuthal) and immanence (tashbih) are identically the same, the Tradition which has been quoted by Āmina Bin Khālid Bin 'Abdullā, both tammathal and tashbih are proved. He will appear in the form of the images they worshipped."[192-193] Similarly Abū Musā Ash'arī cites from tradition:[194] "He will come out in His Glory smilingly" and in Paradise the 'vision will be in the form of Light as cited by Huazifā in: "He will appear before them and cover them in His Light."[195] Finally carefully note the tradition about the Vision in Mi'raj (the Ascension) which Tirmidhī has quoted from Ibn-i-'Abbās:[196] "God appeared in the Glow of His Own Light and (the Prophet) beheld Him twice (in this state).

Besides these self-revelations of Paradise and of the Last Day, it is also proved by some traditions that the Prophet Muḥammad, beheld God Almighty in wakefulness, in a definite form. In this connection note the tradition quoted by Tirmidhī and Dārimī.

"I saw My Lord in a handsome form; He said, "O Muḥammad, what do the Seraphim quarrel about?" I replied, "You know better than myself." "Then He placed His hand between both the shoulder-blades by which I felt coolnes between both the sides of my chest. Thus I discovered all that which is between the heavens and the earth" and then he quoted from the Qur'ān: "Thus did we show Abrahām the Kingdom of the heavens and the earth that he might be of those possessing certainty."[198]

As the 'Kingdom of the heavens and the earth' was unveiled to the Prophet Abrahām in wakefulness only, so the text of the statement shows that Prophet also beheld God Almighty in the best form in wakefulness only.

In dreams, too, the appearance of God is visible. Aḥmad and Tirmidhi quote from Ma'az bin Jabal :[199] "I saw my Lord in the best form." From another tradition of Tirmidhī, 'Abdur Rahmān Bin 'Auf quotes:[200] "I saw my Lord in the form of a beardless youth."

History also supports the view that saints too were gifted with such revelational powers. Accordingly Imām Abū Ḥanīfā beheld God Almighty a hundred times in his visions and Imām Aḥmad Bin Hambal saw God Almighty in a dream and inquired of Him, which form of worship was the best of all. The reply accorded to him was 'the recitation of the Qur'ān'. He queried whether it should be recited in full knowledge of its meaning or without it. Said God: 'Either with meaning or without it.'

After going through all these proofs it could be affirmed that according to Shari'at God's assumption of forms or immanence is an accepted doctrine, but this assuming of forms or immanence does not conflict with His essential transcendence. Note that the *Seraph* Gabriel used to appear before the Prophet Muḥammad in the shape of Haḍrat Daḥyā Kulbī, but such an appearance produced no difference or proved detrimental to the fact of his being an angel of the highest order. Similarly the angel Azraeīl, during the performance of disembodying the soul, appears simultaneously at different places in different shapes, but this change and variety of forms do not produce any alteration or multiplicity in the being of Azraeīl—in its entity and it remains totally unchanged, as it was before. Now probably you might have understood what I have said viz., that God in His Own Immutable State, Attribute and Being without altering His Individuality manifests Himself through His attribute of Light in the forms of phenomenal objects. Probably you will agree with the following statement of Shāh Kamālullāh:[201]

The Categorical word of God affirms :
God manifests Himself in thy form.

God possesses both the attributes of immanence and transcendence. He is the Inward as well as the Outward. The Inward rank is of absolute transcendence (tanzih mutlaq), is the Divine Essence *per se* and *esse* unknown and unknowable, absolute Ghayb (unseen), and immanence (tashbih) is predicated of Him in the stage of manifestation. In the Holy Qur'ān both the Tanzih verses and Tashbih verses are found in plenty. To believe in one and reject the other is the way of those who deny God and His apostles, as indicated by the Qur'ān.[202] In the manifestative phase God has attributed Himself with the attributes of immanence such as hand, face, etc. and according to this attribution of Immanence it is right to say that the hand of the Prophet is the hand of God. The perfection of one's faith depends upon belief in both these attributes i.e., immanence and transcendence, in other words, God is transcendent in His Essence and in manifestations He is immanent. He comprises both immanence and transcendence. He is not merely transcendent in the sense that He may not be immanent as believed by the Ash'arites, as such transcendence, on reflection, would prove to be limitation. Further it would imply that God Almighty is like abstract terms free from space and direction, and if He is pure in this sense, then, He becomes like the abstract principles, though He may not be like corporeal things. It is clear that this is limitation and comparison and not transcendence. God Almighty is not entirely immanent, too, as believed by the corporealist; such as immanence, is also a limitation, and God Almighty is free from all limitation and determination. The right way would be to believe that God Almighty is immanent in His very transcendence i.e. He is manifest with His own purity and transcendence in the likeness of everything, and is transcendent, in His very immanence, because everything that exists is 'dead, is a relative not-being, and God Almighty alone exists, to what could then He be compared? "Everything is, as it were, dead except His own self."[203-204] Shaykh Akbar has beautifully expressed this belief thus:[205]

If you assert (pure) transcendence
you limit God,
And if you assert (pure) immanence
you define Him.

i.e. if you believe only in pure transcendence you would be among those who limit God, in other words, the Being of God would be confined in the unseen and it would necessarily entail the denial of the words 'He is the Outward.' If it is admitted that God is the Inward without admitting that He is the Outward also, it would mean the limitation of His absolute Being. And if you believe in immanence alone then you will be among those who define God, as the admission of the words 'He is the Outward' without the acceptance of the words 'He is Inward' is defining and limiting the Absolute Being; it is, as it were, depriving Him of transcendence and God Almighty cannot thus be defined. Then says the Shaykh:[206]

But if you assert both things you
follow the right cause,
And you are leader and a master in
gnosis.

i. e. if you believe in both the facts and acknowledge that God Almighty is transcendent in His very immanence and is Immanent in His very transcendence you will be on the right path and become the leader and master in Divine Knowledge.

I have expounded above the aspects of identity and otherness in God (Ḥaqq) and created things (Khalq). Remember that the aspect of identity has the same sense which transcendence has, and the aspect of otherness has the same meaning as immanence has. In this connection keep in view clearly the aspects of identity and otherness. Since the essences of created things subsist in the Mind of God, so in accordance with this subsistence, Identity is predicated from the beginning to Eternity. As Jāmī says:[207]

Once we were one with Him, the Lord
of Being.
The question of Being other than He
never, then, did arise !

And as the Being of God (Ḥaqq) is existent, the essences of Created things are "non-existent", (this is relative not-being and not absolute not-being, as explained above) therefore from the point of view of essences, 'otherness' is predicated from the beginning to eternity. As the Ṣūfī postulate is:[208] "The 'Known' of God from Eternity is other than God." There is real disparity between existence and non-existence, Being and Not-Being, consequently, from the point of view of essences 'otherness' is real, and from the point of view of existence or Being "identity" is real, because the existence of God (Ḥaqq) is nothing but the existence of the Created beings, i. e. the same one Being is revealing itself in the forms of the essences of Created things. The right faith depends on the confirmation of both of these relations. Sincerely believing in both identity and otherness is the acquiring of perfect knowledge. S͟hāh Kamāl-ud-din has expressed this idea beautifully in a couplet thus:[209]

To soar in the realm of gnosis,
Develop the twin wings of Identity
and otherness.

Ṣūfīs are firmly convinced that he who is wholly attracted by the phenomenal (i.e. Otherness) is the "Veilest" (Maḥjūb), and he who identifies the phenomenal with God, the Real, or who regards the phenomenal as real, is an 'Illusionist' (Mag͟hzūb), and he who is intoxicated with the wine of Unity is an "absorptionist (Majzūb), and he who clearly distinguishes between the phenomenal and the real, (otherness and identity) and adjusts his relationship therewith accordingly, is the one loved of God, or favoured of Him (Maḥbūb). He does not let the thought of the phenomenal dominate over the thought of the real, and vice versa. His mind displays a happy synthesis of the two, and in the language of Shāh Kamāl he gives expression to this trait of his mind:[210]

Drunk with reality, sober in relation
to everything beside it, (reality).
Every moment a sip of this wine, the
same moment a touch of sobriety,
is all that I need !

"He hath loosed the two seas.[211] They meet. There is a barrier between them. They encroach not (one upon the other). Which is it, of the favours of your Lord, that ye deny ?"[212]

By the knowledge of this 'otherness' and 'identity', the phenomenal and real, immanence and transcendence, we acquire the knowledge of our own self, that God Almighty being free from the aspects of our being is manifesting Himself through the aspects of our being alone. This gnosis grants us the rank of " 'abdiyat" which is the highest position of nearness to God. 'Abdiyat is the knowledge of the fact that:

Firstly, we are supplicants (faqīr): Kingdom and Sovereignty, attributes, actions and existence do not originally belong to us; they belong to God Almighty alone—

"I bear only the name for its own sake,
the rest is He alone."[213]

That is why says the Qurān:[214]

"And Allah is the Rich and ye are the poor."[215]

"O, mankind ! Ye are the Supplicants in your relation to Allah ! He is the All Sufficient, the Owner of Praise."[216-217]

Kingdom and Sovereignty and Command are meant for God Almighty alone:[218]

"The Command rests with none but God."[219]

"Who hath no partner in the Sovereignty."[220-221]

"His are all things in the heavens and on earth."[222-223]

God Almighty Himself is creating actions:[224]

"God has created you and what ye make."

He is asserting positively that there is no other Creator save Him:[225]

"Or do they nssign to God partners who have created (anything) as He has created, so that the Creation seemed to them similar ? Say, "God is the Creator of all things; He is the One, the Supreme and Irresistible.[226]

Attributes belong individually to God only; He alone has existence:[227] "The Living, the Self-Subsisting Eternal."[228] Knowledge and Power are His:[229] "It is He who has knowledge and power."[230] Will and intention belong to Him:[231] "But ye will not except as God wills."[232] Hearing and Seeing pertain to Him:[233] "He is the One who heareth and seeth (all things).[234]

How well this thought is expressed by a poet:[235]

"Do you know who you are and what you are?
Look into your mind and say if you do exist
at all or do not exist.
He that sees is the Seer, He that hears is the
Hearer,
He that knows is the knower, but pray tell
me what after all you are!

It has been also proved that God alone has existence:[236] "God! There is none worthy of worship save God!—The Living, the Self Subsisting, Eternal"[237] and "He is the First and the Last, and the Outward and the Inward, and He is Knower of all things."[238-239] All the four aspects of existence are posited in God Almighty alone. As soon as a gnostic feels this want he involuntarily exclaims:[240]

Whatever is in me is not mine, it is all
Thine,
What do I lose if I present Thee with what
is Thine!

The mystic of Rūm expresses this state thus:[241]

What is to know the Unity of God?
It is to extinguish oneself in presence
of the One
Shouldst thou desire to be as bright as day
Burn out thy Separate existence like the candle
of the night.
Since separate existence brings in violent
inebriation,
Reason forsakes the mind, shame, the heart.
He who loses his separate existence,
The result of what he does is always full
of bliss.

Now, God only is outwardly and inwardly Existent, has Will inwardly and outwardly, and is All-powerful, All-seeing, All-hearing and All-speaking, inwardly and outwardly. This, in the terminology of the gnostics, is called "Proximity of Obligation" (Qurb Farāiḍ), that is from the point of view of 'Existence' (Min ḥaiṯhal Wajūd) 'I do not exist', God (Ḥaqq) alone exists. Ḥaḍrat Kamāl-ullah-Shāh has graphically described this reality in the following couplets:[242]

Bereft of life and knowledge, bereft of
 power and will,
How shall I describe my state? I do not
 exist; He alone exists!
Deaf I am, the Hearer is He: Blind I am;
 the Seer is He,
Dumb I am, the Speaker is He; I do not
 exist, He alone exists!
He is the First, He is the Last, He is the
 Outward, He is the Inward,
Out of sight is He, the ever-present also
 is He; I do not exist, He alone exists!
Eternity is His attribute; Not-Being is my
 reality.
This is so every moment; I do not exist,
 He alone exists!
He was, not I, in the Ever-before, I will
 not be, then, in the Ever-After.
Listen! even now as Ever before in the
 same state is He; I do not exist, He
 alone exists.

Secondly 'abdiyat consists in realising the fact that we are 'trustees' (Amīn). We gain the distinction of 'trusteeship' by means of the distinction of 'want' (faqr). In ourselves are found existence, ego, actions and attributes, etc. by way of a trust. I am existing through the existence of God Almighty Himself, am alive through His life only, I know through His knowledge, I possess will and power through His Will and Power; I hear through His sense of hearing, I see through His Sight and speak through His power of speech. This alone, in the terminology of the Ṣūfis, is the "Proximity of Supererogation" (Qurb-i-Nawāfil). Existence and existential attributes are originally and exclusively posited in God Almighty alone, and they are being associated with us by way of a trust. By knowing the aspects of 'want' (faqr) and 'trust' (amānat) the Qur'ānic concept:[243] "Glory be to Allah—and I am not of the Idolaters"[244] which is the intuition of the Prophet—is realised i.e. we do not assert that the things meant for God Almighty are meant for us originally, and thus we are very far from 'Shirk' i.e. believing in other external existence; neither are we ascribing our things, non-existential attributes etc., to God, which would affect his pure transcendence and necessarily make us infidels (Kāfir). We are asserting His things for Him only and this is real Unification (Tawḥid).

As a consequence of Want and Trust the 'abd is vested with 'Viceregency' and 'Saintship'. When he uses Divine trusts versus the universe, the title of 'Viceregent of God on Earth' is conferred on him, and when he makes use of them in relation to God he is termed 'Saint' (Wali). These only are the four aspects of the 'abd viz. Want, Trust, Viceregency and Saintship. What a dignified being is the 'abd !

In worth you are the Sovereign of both
the worlds ![245]
Pity it is you do not realise your own
worth !

Magrabī describes this dignity thus:[246]

We are reflections of the Essence,
We are manifestations of the totality of
all His Attributes
We are the visage of the Necessary Being !
We are the meaning of the Contingent world !
We are beyond space and yet bound by it.
We are beyond every dimension and yet bound
by all !
*We are the Cure for the Sick !
We are salvation for the weak and
imprisoned!
We are like the Pole Star stead-fast,
stationary

Although like the transient heavens
we revolve !

Another gnostic, keeping in view the dignity of Caliphate and 'Saintship' has said:[247]

We are the pillars and the green dome
We are pivots round which the world of
things revolve !
We are the Circumference and the Centre
and the Revolution
We are an all round Compass of the Being.
We are the occupant of the Throne of
Qāba Qausayn (S.L III,9)
And the two worlds are there on account
of us.

The 'abd has acquired this dignity because he has God with him, he has His Huwiyya and Anniya, His attributes, His actions with him. Consequently the 'abd is Lost to his sense of self-subsistence, loses himself in the Self-Substance of God (in His Huwiyya and Anniyya). "Our existence is from Him and our Subsistence is from Him too".[248] "He alone is and nothing else, and the totality of existence is His only." When the 'abd is dead in relation to his own self, he becomes alive in his relation to the Self of God. Now listen through the lips of a lover what happens to him:[249]

Said the Beloved yesterday, O my Love,
I am one with thee
Only when thou hast shorn thyself of thy
duality !

I then beheld him with his eyes and said:

Who art thou, O thou Life of the World?
Promptly he said: "Thee" (Irāqī)
I said to her, Could I have a look at thee,
O Beauty?
Said she; Shouldst thou care to see me,
go ahead and see thy ownself.
I said; the yearning of my heart is to
dwell with thee !
Said she; if this so, dwell thee with
thine own self !

I said; Will it be right if I talk to thee
discarding the veil between?
Said She; None has ever before talked to
me with a veil between ! (Magrabī)

When the 'abd begins to live in the Essence (Dhāt) of God, the Essence being absolute bliss, the 'abd feels in him an ecstasy which baffles expression and which no worldly sorrow can affect; and he, according to the Qur'ānic Concept.[249] "Verily in the remembrance of Allah do hearts find rest",[250] becomes the abode of bliss and of the peace of mind which passes understanding. As Jāmī says:[251]

Like bulbul I am inebriate with Thee,
My sorrows grow from memories of Thee,
Yet all earth's joys are dust beneath
the feet
Of those entrancing memories of Thee.[252]
In the state of separation I felt sad
and distressful,
In union I felt my self-consciousness and
my self-hood had bereft me !
Joy came to dwell in my soul
And now do I keep my body and soul
in a state of bliss !

The verse:[253] "But ah ! thou soul at peace ! Return unto thy Lord, content in His good pleasure ! Enter thou among My bondmen ! Enter thou My Garden"[254] is now aptly applicable to him and he steps into Paradise.

2 The knowledge and actions of the 'abd follow from the knowledge and actions of God. Self and lust are annihilated. The 'abd realises that how could he possess knowledge who does not have existence by himself and how could his actions be his own. According to his aptitude knowledge and action are created by God Himself. He finds that Knowledge, whether it may pertain to guidance or to misguidance, is born out of self; but he knows this, too, that knowledge is the attribute of the Knower alone, and the Knower is God Himself. In the Essence and attributes of God disparity and separability are neither conceivable by reason nor by religion nor by mystical illumination. Therefore, God Almighty is substantiated in

Selves, and we understand the meaning of "Thus Allah sendeth astray whom He will and whom He will He guideth."[255-256] The knowledge of guidance and misguidance contained in the selves is imparted by God Himself according to the aptitude of the 'abd. The 'abd considers that in his actions he is guided by God and he does not think that he could be the Creator of his acts.

Your 'Self' is non-existent, knowing one ![257]
Deem not your actions by yourself are done;
Make no wry faces at this wholesome truth,
Build the wall ere the fresco is begun.[258]

The 'abd feels the immediate Presence of God within, senses the Presence of God without. He sees God reflected in every face, back of every countenance, moving in every act. With Maghrabī he cries out:[259]

Whithersoever my eye turns, it beholds
    Him only,
Whatever it sees it sees Him along with it.
Others look at Him only from one angle;
    I look at Him from all angles.
They approach Him from one side only;
    I approach Him from all sides.
Sometimes I find Him through the phenomenal world;
    sometimes I find the phenomenal world through Him.
At one moment, as it were, everything is He;
    at another, everything is from Him.
O Maghrabī, He whom thou seekest in thy
    sanctum
I but only behold Him in every lane and street.

And sometimes agreeing with Shaykh Akbar says:[258]

The eye does not see anything except God,
Predication of everything is of Him only.
So we are wholly His; we owe our being to
    Him; we are completely in His hand;
And in every station we are with Him.

And in the words of his Master Muḥammad, the Prophet, desires to be blessed with the joy of His Sight:[259]

"O Allah ! Bless me always with the joy of thy sight and the pleasure of beholding thy countenance, unharmed by anything harmful and undisturbed by anything disturbing !"[260]

He feels the Presence of God in him, not even for a moment is he oblivious of His Presence. Every moment he feels God within (Yāft) and senses God without (Shahūd). Any absence of this dual sense experience is galling to him. He does not care for all the other objects, he is independent of all things and not dependent on anything. He acts on the Qurānic injunction:"[261] "Ye grieve not for the sake of that which hath escaped you, nor yet exult because of that which hath been given."[262] Addressing the Veilist he says:[263]

O thou who wanderest in search of God,
Thou must indeed be blind since thou
art seeking Him out of thyself !
God tells thee through the tongue of everything,
From thy head to foot it is Me, where,
then, thou wanderest in search of Me ?

At times he addresses them thus:[264]

O, thou who seekest God in every nook
and corner !
Thou art indeed God Himself, not anything
beside !
This quest of thine is like the quest
Of water drop in the ocean which may like
to seek the ocean !

He is reminded of the times of his quest and repeats the words which had issued from his lips at the end of the quest:[265]

O Friend, I sought for Thee in all places,
And asked of thy whereabouts from every passer by !
I saw me with thee and found thee was
really me !
It was a shame that I searched for thee !
O Friend, how long this gulf between thee
and me !
When I am really thee how long this talk
of me and thee ?

Since thy self-respect does not admit of
existences other than Thine
Why keep up this pretence of separation?

So the work of a real 'abd is to feel God within and to sense God without. The outcome of it is 'Effacement in the Essence of God' [Maḥwiat fiz Dhāt—] i.e. when one is absorbed in God with complete abstraction from self, the signs of the 'Huwal Bāṭin' (He is the Inward) make their appearance. This stage is what the Ṣūfis call the 'total passing away' [fanā-al-fanā], is complete effacement, is a 'retrocession of trust' (Isterdād-i-amānat). Now the 'abd does not exist, God is all in all.

God stayed back, the rest passed away ![266]
By God! nothing exists save God!
But :[267]
Don't you make any mistake. Mark :
He who has lost himself in God does
not himself become God.

"Say Allah:[268] "Then leave them."[269] But this is what the Prophet hinted at: "I have sometimes a moment in God which neither the most intimate angels of God nor his Messengers can attain thereto."[270] It is not in his power, this is a state (ḥāl) not a stage (Maqām). His position is really that of an 'abd which is the highest stage of Nearness or Proximity. Note that due to this only the Prophet has been addressed as 'abd in the Ascension (Mi'rāj) and this appellation denotes his closest contact and nearness to God:[271] "Glorified be He who carried His '*abd* by night."[272] And He revealed unto His '*Abd* that which he revealed."[273]-[274] For the same reason his consummated place is 'abdiyat. He considers devotion, worship or service as obligatory. In sobriety an 'abd cannot free himself from the trammels of S̲harī'at (the Law). The mystic of Rūm describes the wisdom contained in it thus:[275]

Despite his nearness to God
He does not cease to exert himself towards Him.
If the guide who knows the right from the wrong,
Does not keep to the right stead-fastly himself,
How can he rescue humanity from its sorrows?

It is because the Leader is steadfast in his action,
Those behind him feel inclined to follow his example.
Further, Divine splendour has no limits,
And God discloses Himself every moment in fresh Glory.
Since the Known is not finite,
Knowledge necessarily is without bounds.
Should he keep on striving,
And spend his days and nights in devotion,
Every momemt he beholds a fresh aspect of His beauty.
Necessarily, therefore, he has ever to be on the move !
Look at the Prophet ! Despite his greatness,
The Lord of Majesty cautions him: "Stand upright !"
The function of guidance becomes the adept,
Who dead to self lives in Him.
He alone will be the true Guide on the Path of Reality
Who himself observes the Law.
Seek out such an adept if you care to pursue the Path,
That is the only way to share the company of your Friend !

Even if all the worldly possessions are bestowed on the devotee of God, he would not even cast a glance on them, because he knows the real state of affairs:[276]

Turn wheresoever thou mayst,
In the end thou wilt have to dive into the bosom.
Say, is there anyone better than He
Who can give you bliss even for a moment ?
Neither joy nor power do I seek,
What I desire of thee is thee alone !

The Life Aim of a true devotee is devotion of this type only, a devotion expressive of absolute dependence on God, a devotion which alone offers the Bliss Consciousness that he needs in the world :[277]

The urge of my life is to serve thee only!
For the God-Conscious a moment without
thee is verily a sin !
Everyone asks of thee whatever his heart desires,
What Jāmī, however, asks of thee is
nothing but thee alone !
What he asks of his Master is just this :[278]

"O Lord, thou art my Goal, and I desire nothing but thy pleasure. I have discarded for thee the present and the world to follow. Complete thy favour on me and grant me thy closest Nearness !"

Such a devotee enters the ranks of those whom God has drawn near and entitles himself to the divine approbation:[279]

"There is for him Rest,
Peace and a Garden of Bliss."[280]

CHAPTER IV

"TANAZZULĀT"

THE DESCENT OF THE ABSOLUTE

The essential modes in earth and heavens present
Facets of Him who's veiled and immanent;[1]
Hence, O inquirer, learn what essence is
What attribute, what cause, what consequent.[2]

When in His partial modes Truth shone out plain,
Straightway appeared this world of loss and gain;[3]
Were it and all who dwell there gathered back
Into the whole, the Truth would still remain.[4]

In the preceding chapter, offering an explanation of the correlation between God (Ḥaqq) and the created things (Khalq) I had remarked that the essences of the created things are created externally and known internally; they are 'other' than the Being of God. The Being of God is free and exempt from all those aptitudes which belong to the essences of Created things. Thus 'Otherness' of the essences, is definitely established. The Qur'ān and the Traditions support and confirm it. They further make it clear that the 'inward' and 'outward' of the essences of the created beings is God (Ḥaqq). Their first and last is God, He is immanent in them, is with them and He is near to them. In spite of 'Otherness', the explanation of this "identity" (i.e. firstness, lastness, nearness, proximity, immanence and omnipresence) as we have proved, could be given in this way that 'God in His own Immutable State, Attribute and Being without altering His Individuality, manifests Himself through His Attribute of Light in the forms of phenomenal objects, which in reality are but reflected entities, expressing outwardly the essences which subsist in the Knowledge of God and hence it is that the Divine Aspects (Being, Attributes etc.) came to be associated with the world of creation or phenomena.'

Making the Qur'ān and the Traditions the criterion of truth we have proved this statement by that which the text of the Qur'ān clearly denotes without any sort of *interpretation* [tāwīl] of the text. Further we supported and confirmed it by authentic Traditions.

The same stupendous truth has been presented by the Ṣūfīs in their difficult technical writings. This has been spoken of as the Theory of the "Tanazzulāt-e-Sittā." It is a famous and well-known theory; many treatises have been written on it which explain and make it lucid. By giving a summary of this theory, here, I desire to show that the eminent Ṣūfīs at some places explained some points with a great deal of detail and did not explain some points at all, with the result that numerous misunderstandings arose leading to a host of controversies and subsequently to ibāḥat [regarding everything as permissible] and atheism as well and disturbed the faith of so many people. The athcists and heretics began to preach of pure 'identity', and denied the 'otherness' of things. The Qur'ān and the Traditions were no longer the criterion of truth ! This preaching was regarded as an arcane secret which was being transferred from one person to another orally [Ilm-i-Sinā] and in which there was not the slightest possibility of an error. According to this knowledge imparted orally, 'identity' and not 'otherness' of things' is the truth; a thing is not 'other' than the Being of God, it is nothing but the Being of God. "The Unity of Being" [Waḥdatu'l-Wujūd] or 'Everything is He' [hama oost is not according to the Being, it is according to the thing. There is no need to follow S͟harī'at (The Law). So long as there is 'otherness', there is S͟hrī'āt and when otherness is denied and identity proved and God (Ḥaqq) alone remained, where is the necessity of following S͟hrī-'at ? S͟hrī'at and reality are two separate and opposite departments, there is no harmony between the two. That which is lawful in S͟harī'at is unlawful in Tarīqat and conversely that which is lawful in Tarīqat is unlawful in S͟harī'at. So long as there was ignorance we were, as it were, tied with the chains of S͟harī'at. No sooner did we gain the Knowledge of Tarīqat than the secret of reality was revealed to us; ignorance was dispelled, and we acquired freedom. 'Abdiyat, want, trust, vicegerency and saintship are meaningless words. God is All in All, God is everything. This is the sum and substance of their knowledge of self, knowledge of the Prophet and knowledge of God. Their Ancients had said 'Our system of doctrine is firmly bound up with the dogmas of Faith, the Qur'ān and the Traditions' (Junayd[5]), now they claim that the criterion of truth of this verbal knowledge is neither the Qur'ān nor the Traditions. The prayer of their predecessors was :[6]

"I expect to be one of those who strictly
follow the Law and to be raised up
among the followers of the Prophet, as we
in our lives are numbered among his people."

Now they regard Sharī'at as the chains of their feet and think that they have discovered the mystery of the universe and this discovery has released them from the bonds of the Prophet's Sharī'at !

At the outset grasp thoroughly the theory of Tanazzulāt. This will clear up the ambiguities which have been the cause of this heresy and atheism. The clarification of this ambiguity will put an end to all misunderstandings and misguidance.

Real Being (Wujūd) belongs to God Almighty alone. "God is the Absolute Being."[7]

There are two fundamentally different senses in which the term 'Being' may be understood:

(i) It may mean "Being" as a concept: The idea of "Being"; Existence.[8]

(ii) It may mean that which has being, i.e. that which exists or subsists.

As Jāmī explains :

"Taken in the first sense, 'being' is an "idea of the second intention"[10] which has no external object corresponding with it. It is one of the accidents of the 'quidity' (or real nature of the thing) which exists only in thought, as has been proved by the reasonings of Scholastic theologians and philosophers.

"In the Second sense 'Being' signifies the Real Being, who is Self-existent, and on whom the existence of all other beings depends; and in truth there is no real objective existence beside Him—all other beings are merely accidents accessory to Him, as is attributed by the intuitive apprehension of the most famous Gnostics and 'men of certitude'. The word 'Being' is applicable to God in the latter sense only.

> Things that exist to men of narrow view
> Appear the accidents to substance due;[11]
> To men of light substance is accident
> Which the 'True Being' ever doth renew."[12]

God is Absolute Being. He has no partner, no equal. Neither His opposite nor His like exists. He possesses neither form nor shape. Neither has He an origin nor an end; neither is He universal nor particular. He is free and exempt from all limitations, even free from the limitation of absoluteness (qayd-i-iṭlāq). Intuitive apprehension by which He is apprehended is 'supra-rational' and not 'contra-rational.' *Theoretical* premises can neither affirm Him nor deny Him. According to the Qur'ānic text "He is not in the likeness of anything."[13] He is free from all the aspects of the created beings and consequently absolutely transcendent.

What is God, the Absolute Being Himself, according to His origin and essential nature ? The senses, thought, reason and understanding are at a loss to find Him, because all of the above faculties are temporal and contingent, and contingent can perceive the contingent only. Hence it is the greatest philosophers who are baffled by the impossibility of attaining to the knowledge of His Essence. His first characteristic is the lack of all characteristics and the last result of the attempt to know Him is stupefaction.

> "However great our heavenly knowledge be
> It cannot penetrate Thy sanctuary;[14]
> Saints blest with vision and with light divine
> Reach no conceptions adequate to Thee !"[15]
> Here the climax of perception is the inability to perceive.

"Admission of inability to perceive is itself a sort of perception."[16]-[17]

The destination reached by perception would be the object of perception itself and not God.

As Rūmī has said :

You cannot visualise for yourself any path beyond the utmost reaches of your vision.[18]

The utmost reaches possible for reason's quest can certainly not be God (who is beyond the grasp of reason).

The philosophers who tried to discover the origin and essential nature of God, have truly speaking wasted their time. "No one knows God except God Himself."[19]

Now, the same Absolute Being that in the stage of transcendence is unknown and unknowable reveals Himself in multiple manifestations and different forms, or in the terminology of eminent Ṣūfīs, descends in these forms, or individualises Himself in different forms. This is of such a nature that in spite of expressing Himself in different manifestations and multiple forms the Absolute Being maintains His immutable State, Attributes and Being and no change of any kind does necessarily take place. The stages of descent are innumerable but the most marked of these are but six and these are termed the Six Descents by the Ṣūfīs. The first three of them are called, 'Marātib-i-Ilāhi' (Divine ranks) which are 'Aḥadiyyat' (Abstract Oneness) i.e. the state of the Essence, the colourless, the infinite, the indeterminate. The second is 'Waḥdat' (Unity) and the third 'Wāḥidīyyat' (Unity in Plurality).[20-21] The remaining three are called 'Marātib-i-Kawnī (Worldly ranks) which are 'Ruḥ' (Spirit), 'Mit͟hāl' (similitude) and 'Jism' (body). 'Man' comes last of all these and his rank is inclusive of all the other ranks. Since Aḥadiyyat is the state of pure Being, therefore there are six descents from Waḥdat or the first descent to the state of man. Leaving off man there are five states from the state of first descent to the state of body; these are called the Five Planes of Being. The following Table will explain some of the technical terms and the order of the states :[22]

1	2	3	4	5	6	7
First Plane	Second Plane	Third Plane	Fourth Plane	Fifth Plane	Sixth Plane	Seventh Plane
Dhāt—state of the Essence.	First descent	Second descent	Third descent	Fourth descent	Fifth descent	Sixth descent

1	2	3	4	5	6	7
Aḥadiyyat State of Unity	Waḥdat	Waḥidiy-yat	Spirit	Simili-tudes	Body	Man
Inward	Reality of Muhammad	A'yān-āl-Thābitā				

1 to 3 Divine ranks 4 to 6 Worldly ranks

2 to 6 Five Planes of Being

2 to 3 Manifes-tation in Knowledge 4 to 7: External manifestation

2 to 7: Six Descents.

Now I think it necessary to explain in detail some points of the above Descents.

"Beware ! Lest you lose your way and go astray."

(1) *Aḥadiyyat* : The state of Abstract Unity, Aḥadiyyat implies the Absolute Being of God. As I have said above, this Being according to His essential nature is unknown and unknowable, that is the reason why He is spoken of as the "Absolute Ghayb" (unseen). This is defined by Ṣūfīs on lines which may fairly be represented by the words of Jīlī in his Insān-i-Kāmil. 'The Essence means the Absolute dropping all modes, adjuncts, relations and aspects. Not that they are external to the Absolute Being but that all these modes and what is ascribed to them are totally of and in the Absolute Being, not of themselves nor by nature of their own modes, but essentially one with the Absolute. And this Absolute Being is the pure Essence in which there is no manifestation, no name, no quality, no relation, no adjunct, or anything else. So when anything else is manifested in it that manifestation is ascribed not to the Pure Essence but to that which is manifested. Then the Essence in the requirement of its own nature comprises Universals, Particulars, Relations and Adjuncts by the requirement of their countenance. Nay, by the requirement of their disappearance beneath the domination of the Oneness of the Essence."[23] "God was and there was naught beside Him"[24] refers to the same state. Aḥadiyyat is a state of the colourless, the state of the Essence. Consequently, the desire to acquire gnosis is of no

avail; reference is being made to this in the Qur'ān: "But they shall not compass Him with their knowledge."[25-26] "Allah biddeth you beware of Him."[27-28] The Prophet Muḥammad had said about it: "I have not known thee to the extent that thy knowledge demands"[29] and had warned the thinkers thus: "Don't indulge in speculating on the nature of God lest ye may be destroyed."[30] As the outcome of thinking is gnosis and the gnosis of the Essence of God is impossible, so the consequences of the quest for the impossible would be death. 'Aṭṭār says :[31]

Why exert to probe the Essence of God ?
Why strain thyself by stretching thy limitations ?
When thou canst not catch even the essence of an atom,
How canst thou claim to know the Essence
of God Himself ?

All the other names given to the 'state of Unity' (Aḥadiyyat) by the eminent Ṣūfīs show that the gnosis of the Essence of God is utterly impossible. Reflect on a few of them: 'Ghayb-al-Ghayūb (the Unseen of the Unseen) : Munqaṭa' al-Wijdān (the Incommunicable); Ghayb-i-Huwiyyat; 'Ayn-i-Muṭlaq (the Absolute Essence); Maknūn-al-Muknūn (the Hidden of all Hidden Beings); Manqaṭa-'al-Ishārāt (One of whom all indications are dropped); Wujūd-i-baḥat (Pure Existence); Dhat-i-Sādhij (Colourless Reality); 'Ayn-al-Kāfūr (fountain of camphor i. e. whatever enters into camphor becomes camphor itself). This is agnosticism. It has been expressed by Shaykh Muhyid Dīn-Ibnul'Arabī in these words:[32] "We are all fools in the matter of the gnosis of the Essence of God." Ḥafiz says :[33]

Take off your net; you can't catch 'Unqā
For that will be like attempting to catch the air !

So we should repeat the above couplet and keep away from this "illegitimate thinking" (Fikr-i-ḥarām) and busy ourselves in "legitimate thinking" (Fikr-i-ḥalīl), that is thinking about the attributes of God. At some other place Shaykh Akbar says: "To reflect on the Essence of God is not possible. What is, however, possible is to reflect over His world of creation." The gnostic of Rūm lays stress on it thus:[34]

What is called speculation in respect
of the Divine Essence
Is in reality no speculation of the kind whatsoever.
It is self-delusion: for on the road to God
Hundreds of thousands of obstacles interpose ![35]

Waḥdat—(Unity): When the gnostic contemplates the Being of God as One who is conscious of Himself and cognizant of all the potentialities of His Essence summarily, that He alone exists, no one save Him exists and He has the potentiality of manifesting Himself, then this plane is called Waḥdat or the First Epiphany or Determination, or the Reality of Muḥammad (al-haqiqata'l Muḥammadiyya). This plane is also spoken of an "Absolute I". Here four hypostases, which are purely potentialities of the Essence and do not possess existential multiplicity, are implied:

1. Existence (Wujūd) 2. Knowledge ('Ilm)
3. Light (Nūr) 4. Observance (Shuhūd)

God exists. He is conscious of His Being, actions and attributes. He is self-revealing and self-manifest and thus Observant of His own Being. These hypostases are spoken of as Dhātī (pertaining to the Essence) because they cannot be regarded as attributes. In other words they are Essence itself and not super-imposition on the Essence. For if:[36]

1. Existence be regarded as an attribute of Dhat) Essence), it would necessarily imply that the Essence has precedence over Existence. The precedence or priority of the Essence over existence would mean that the Essence exists without existence, which is self-evidently impossible. Therefore it is clearly evident that existence is nothing but the Essence itself and not the attribute of the Essence. Similarly:—

2. Knowledge, too, is identical with the Essence, as the perfection of knowledge consists in encompassing its known; but the Divine Essence is infinite, unlimited, for if it be limited by knowledge it could not be regarded as infinite, unlimited. Consequently knowledge will have to be admitted as identical with the Essence. [Of course, knowledge, too, when compared with contingent beings is unlimited but in comparison

with Pure Essence it cannot be admitted to be unlimited]. In the same way:

3. Light (Nūr) also is identical with the Essence and not the attribute of the Essence. Similarly:

4. Observance (Shuhūd) too, would self-evidently be regarded as identical with the Essence. Thus, in this stage the Essence would be itself 'existence' and the existent and the one which is conscious of its existence; it would be itself the Knower, the Known and the Knowledge; it would itself be the Lighter, the Lighted and the Light and itself the Observer, the Observed and the Observance.

In the four hypostases all the attributes of the Divine and mundane names are included, 'as the whole is included in the inwardness of the Essence, as the detailed is in the totality and as the tree is comprised in the stone'.

The eminent Ṣūfīs have given several names to this Plane. Reflection on them would reveal further meanings to you.

It is called the "First Illumination" [Tajallī-i-Awwal], because it has manifested itself from the stage of inwardness or an indeterminate state. It is called the "First Aptitude" [Qābiliat-i-Awwal], as it is the matter of all the creatures and phenomena, and all the aptitudes reveal themselves through it alone. For the same reason it is spoken of as the "First Existence" [Wujūd-i-Awwal]; "the First Existent" [Mawjūd-i-Awwal]: "the Primary Source" [Mabdā'i-Awwal]; "the First Symbol" [Nishān-i-Awwal]; "the Treasure of Treasurers" [Kanz-al-Kunūz]; "the Treasure of attributes etc." [Kanz-al-Ṣifāt]. On the same grounds it is also termed Maqām Ijmālī; "the First Substance" [Jawhar-i-Awwal]; "the First Thought" [Khayāl-i-Awwal] and "the First Ego" [Anā-i Awwal].

According to the 'First Epiphany' the "Dhāt-i-Ahadiyyat" is called "the Reality of Muḥammad" in the terminology of the eminent Ṣūfīs. The manifestation of the Real Unity [Aḥadiyyat] is the Reality of Muḥammad, all the rest of the ranks of the existents are manifestation of the Reality of Muḥammad. Besides, the Reality of Muḥammad is called the First Reason which is the Supreme Spirit[6] [ar-rūhu'l-a' zum]. The Traditions: "The first thing which God created was reason;"[1] "The first thing which God created was the Light of the Prophet;"[2] "The first thing which God created was my spirit"[3] support it. The same First Reason which includes all the realities of things has been given the different names of "the Book of books," "the Holy Ghost", "the Sublime Spirit," etc. etc.

Why is the Plane of Waḥdat or the First Epiphany called the 'Reality of Muḥammad'? In the following paragraphs you will find that in all the essences of the created beings the relation of the Absolute Ego [and its existence, knowledge, light, observance] is uniform but there is the difference of the manifestation of absoluteness [iṭlāq]. In the human essences this manifestation is more than what it is in the essences of things. That is why it is said that man is a manifestation of the Essence, and all the things, the manifestations of Names. Now, among human individuals the essence of the Prophet Muḥammad is the Perfect Manifestation, consequently he is pre-eminent among all the prophets and is the Last of the Prophets. It means that the manifestation of the Absolute Ego and Its aptitudes here is perfect. For the same reason the Divine Being [which is another name for 'Waḥdat'] is spoken of as the Reality of the essence of Muḥammad and thus the other name given to Waḥdat was 'the Reality of Muḥammad'. Here the thing which should be noted well is that Dhāt [Essence] of Muḥammad and the Reality of Muḥammad are two totally different realities. The Dhāt [essence] of Muḥammad is the 'Known' and the Reality of Muḥammad the 'Knower;' to regard these two as one is, as it were, regarding the 'known' as the 'Knower', the 'Knower' as the 'Known' and the 'abd as the Lord and the Lord as the 'abd. It is, as it were, regarding the possible as the Necessary and the Necessary as the possible. This is clearly 'blasphemy'! [Kufr]. As the Qur'ān says:[37] "In blasphemy indeed are those that say that God is Christ, the son of Mary."[38]

The Dhāt (or Essence) of Jesus Christ is not the Dhāt (or Essence) of God and the Dhāt of Muḥammad is not the Dhāt of God Almighty. Falling a prey to this fallacy and pretending to be the devotees of the Prophet Muḥammad, the ignorant strayed away from the path of reverence and took to worshipping Muḥmmad. Thus, they themselves went astray and misled hundreds of people.

The plane of Waḥdat or Reality of Muḥammad is also termed the "Light of Muḥammad" ['an-nūru'l Muḥammadī]. This too, could be explained as was the Reality of Muḥammad interpreted. Since the idea of Muḥammad is entirely perfect, so perfect Light [which is a hypostasis of the Absolute Ego] manifests itself in it and things are created by this perfect Light only. Therefore, it is said that from the Light of Muḥammad all things were created.[39] "I am from the Light of God and the whole world is from my light" (Ḥadith[40])

Wāḥidiyyat: When the gnostic contemplates the Essence of God in the sense that It possesses knowledge in all its details covering Its Names, Attributes and Ideas together with all their aspects and their interrelationships and their mutual distinctions, this plane is styled Wāḥidiyyat or the Second Epiphany or Reality of Humanity—the Holy Breath.

The only difference between Aḥadiyyat or the First Epiphany and Wāḥidiyyat or the Second Epiphany, is that of totality and its details. Detail is a (sort of) perfection of compendious knowledge and compendious knowledge is the basis of detailed knowledge. Compendious knowledge is preferable to detail, that is the reason why the first plane is styled the plane of 'knowledge' and the second 'the external plane.'

The Plane of Aḥadiyyat is called absolute, the plane of Waḥdat is termed 'implicit' and the Plane of Wāhidiyyat 'explicit'. Waḥdat is an intermediate plane between Aḥadiyyat and Wāḥidiyyat and in this way combines in itself these two great planes, and is therefore called the 'Great Intermediary Plane' (Barzkh-i-Kūbrā).

At this stage, keep in view the three hypostases of Existence referred to above: i) Absolute Waḥdat "without condition of anything" (lābi sharṭ-i shay), indeterminate concept of pure Being i.e. absolute Being, free from both limitation and absoluteness and exempt from transcendence and immanence. ii) Aḥadiyyat—'with condition of nothing', (Bisharṭ-i-la shay) i.e. free and exempt from all limitations and modes. Now we find two alternatives in 'Bisharṭ-i-Shay'—i.e. "with condition of a thing:" potential plurality, this is Waḥdat, and actual plurality, this is Wāḥidiyyat.

Before further explaining iii) Wāḥidiyyat i.e. the third plane, it is necessary to make it clear that all these three planes viz., Aḥadiyyat, Wāhidiyyat and Waḥdat, which are called the "Divine Ranks," are identical with one another. These are suppositional ranks established from the view-point of the gnostic. Temporal distinction is never found in them because it is evident that the Absolute Being could never be conceived at any moment as devoid of knowledge. God Almighty is never unaware of His own Essence, Attributes, Names and Ideas; neither can there be implicitness and explicitness in His absolute knowledge. Therefore the absoluteness of Essence and attributes which was found before the manifestation of things is there even after the manifestation of things. "He is now as He was" (Alān Kamā kān).

Now, let us see the reason why the eminent Ṣūfīs have made the distinction between these ranks. They have justified this distinction from two points of view:

(1) From the rational point of view:

Reason demands that the Essence should exist first and the attributes later. This priority is of rank, not of time. Reason cannot form a conception of attributes without the conception of essence; consequently, the Essence is conceived prior to the attributes, logically and not temporally. Therefore:—

(*a*) The conception of Essence regardless of its attributes is styled 'Aḥadiyyat.' The same has been spoken of as 'pure concept',—'with condition of nothing.' It is understood that this has been referred to in the Qur'ān as: "Say: He is God, the One and only."[41]

(*b*) In respect of attributes the gnostic views them first in their totality or in one sweep and then in detail, one by one. In view of this, Absolute Being in relation to His total attributes is Waḥdat, as indeterminate i.e. with potential plurality and—

(*c*) The Absolute Being with the relation of detailed attributes is Wāḥidiyyat,—'with condition of a thing' i.e. with actual plurality. Says God:[42]

"Your God is one God; there is no God save Him, the Beneficient, the Merciful."[43]

(2) From the point of view of Knowledge and Immediate Vision.

The gnostic gifted with perfect knowledge knows that knowledge is included in essence and the known are included in knowledge. From the point of view of indirāj (entry of one object into another in its highest aspect) knowledge, knower and known are identical; it can never be said that they are the other of one another. But according to the distinction of knowledge, the essence of the Knower has priority over his knowledge and the details of knowledge are the ideas, 'known objects'. This alone is the source of the distinction of the planes of Aḥadiyyat, Wāḥdat and Wāḥidiyyat.

At the time of ascension in knowledge, the eye of a gnostic falls on the world of multiplicity, then, surveying plurality and multiplicity, it turns towards totality and observes Waḥdat (Unity) in multiplicity. When a gnostic buries himself entirely in the observance of Waḥdat the illumination of the Essence (tajalli-i-Dhāt) dawns on him and absorbs him in itself and knowledge and observance that distinguish him are annihilated and he passes away from what belongs to him and persists through what belongs to God. When he returns to consciousness, he styles this stage 'the Unseen of the Unseen' (Ghayb-al-Ghayb). This is the plane of Aḥadiyyat which on account of negation of knowledge disappears from observance. Due to his own presence and absence, a gnostic distinguishes in the Divine ranks and includes points in time, totality and details, presence and absence in them; but Reality is free from all these aspects. His is the only Essence (Dhāt) that every moment manifests Himself through all these three illuminations—where points in time have no place at all.

Shaykh Ibrāhim Shattārī in his work—"Ā'ina-i-Ḥaqayiq" which is a key to 'Jām-i-Jahān-nūmā'[44] comments on the above thus:

"No one should conjecture that the perfection of the Essence found its way in the plane of the First Epiphany—that it was first latent and manifested itself later, or was non-existent before and came into existence afterwards, or that it was missing and made its appearance later, because from these matters it necessarily follows that Existence is imperfect. In fact whatever Existence possesses 'from eternity to eternity' is due to Its perfection alone. Here there is no possibility of any loss, as all the ranks of God are eternal and are necessary for His Essence; they are never separated from His Essence. Reasoning in this stage is helpless; it cannot definitely assert anything; it guesses and says if in the stage of Indetermination the determination of names and attributes is found, there would then be no difference between the two. It is said that this conjecture in the stage of reasoning is valid, but in the stage of absoluteness (iṭlāq) it would be held null and void, because the description of unity and plurality, absolute and relative is given for the benefit of the seekers. Really this is not the case that first there was unity and later it became multiplicity or that there was Absolute first and ultimately became limited. God Almighty's Being is over and above all these matters; He is the same now as He was before."

In the plane of Wāhidiyyat actual plurality is taken into consideration and plurality connotes names, attributes and Divine ideas.

The Absolute Essence (Dhāt) or the Essence of God cannot manifest Itself without attributes. The Essence could be discovered by attributes alone. Attribute signifies the manifestation of the Essence, as the Essence is unlimited, so attributes, too, are infinite and innumerable. When the Essence is qualified by an attribute It is called a name [Ism], names connote the Essence together with Its attributes. Knowledge is the attribute of the Essence, 'Knower' ['Alīm] is a name, life is an attribute of the Essence, the Living [Ḥayy] is a name. Out of the innumerable names the knowledge of ninety-nine has been bestowed on man. Divine attributes, are according to their source and origin, identical with the Essence, that is, they are abstracted from the one Essence alone, only one Essence is their source. "The attributes are distinct from the Essence in thought but are identical with It in fact and reality.... Doubtless just as these attributes are distinct from each other in idea, according to their respective meanings, so they are distinct from the Essence; but in fact and reality they are identical with It. In other words, there are not in It many existences, but only one sole existence and its various names and attributes are merely its modes and aspects.

Pure is the Essence from deficiency
Expressed its "how" and "here" can
never be;[45]
The attributes appear distinct but are,
One with thy essence in reality."[46]

The multiplicity of names and attributes does not cause multiplicity in the Essence. Plurality would have been caused only when they had been admitted to be external existences and independent of the Essence. Names and attributes are only the modes and aspects of the Essence. All of them are abstracted from one Essence only and they subsist in one Essence alone. In the stage of Essence they are called 'potentialities' (Shuyūn), in the stage of knowledge they are termed a'yān, and in the world of phenomena, 'Created beings' (Khalq). Thus neither the plurality of 'eternal beings' nor the plurality of 'necessary beings' is necessitated. Here the Heretics and the Mu'tazilites have blundered badly by denying the existence of the Divine names and their mutual distinction. Here we are led to think of those commentators of Spinoza who even denied to admit the attributes of the Substance, because according to them, the Indeterminate Essence qualified by these attributes becomes limited and finite. But when Spinoza calls God an *ens-absolute indeterminatum*, he does not mean that God is an absolutely indeterminate being, or non-being or negative being, but on the contrary, that He has absolutely *unlimited* attributes or absolutely *infinite* perfections—that He is a positive, concrete, most real being, the being who unites in Himself all possible attributes and possesses them without limitation. By ascribing to God "*infinite attributa*" Spinoza meant that God has both infinite attributes and infinity of attributes."[47]

Ṣūfīs have pointed out seven differences between the Essence and the attributes. Shāh Kamāluddin has presented them in a poem in his collection of verses:

1. The Essence ranks first, the attributes come next (this precedence is logical or of rank).

2. The Essence is self-existing and the attributes depend on the Essence (like wax and its softness).

3. The Essence is unity and the attributes display diversity.

4. The Essence has self-consciousness, (Anniyat), the attributes have none.

5. The Essence is always hidden, the attributes are sometimes hidden and sometimes manifest.

6. The attributes must be in their proper locus.

7. The manifestation of one attribute conflicts with or suppresses the manifestation of another.

After grasping these points the difference between the Essence and the attributes becomes clear. Remember, to posit an attribute in an attribute would be nonsense. e.g. we cannot say that the attribute of joy is the joyous one itself, neither could any attribute be affirmed in a collection of attributes of which this itself is an instance e.g. when we say John is happy we do not or cannot mean that the attributes which constitute the nature of John are happy themselves, whether these attributes are viewed individually or collectively. In short we cannot, like the Empiricists, assert that attributes alone exist and the essence does not exist at all. One who makes this assertion has to admit the nonsense that attributes could be predicated of attributes only—that attributes alone are the bearers of attributes. The existence of essence is imperative—an essence which without itself becoming an attribute possesses attributes. Now after noting the difference between the essence and the attribute, reflect once more on the distinctions which have been presented by the eminent Ṣūfīs and which have been given above.

It has been shown that in the plane of Waḥdat four aspects of it, viz., Existence, light, knowledge and observance, which are merely an aptitude of essence and have no existential plurality, have already come up for consideration. Now in the stage of Wāḥidiyyat Essence becomes 'existence' (life), knowledge absolute (of self) becomes knowledge of attributes or love. Light becomes will and S͟hhūd becomes power. Life, knowledge, will and power are Primary Attributes or mothers of attributes. They comprise all the attributes of Divinity. From these alone are brought forth three more attributes which are hearing, sight and speech. You may, if you prefer, say that the Primary Attributes are seven, viz., life, knowledge, will, power, hearing, sight and speech.

In names and attributes, the source of all attributes is Life. It is regarded as the 'Imām-al-Āyymmā' (the leader of all leaders). The Name al-Ḥayy ("The Living") is the predecessor of all names and the words, Seer, Hearer, Knower, the Determiner, the one who wills (al-murīd) and the Speaker explain the name al-'Hayy' only.

The name, 'The Knower' (al-'Alīm) rules over all the names and all the words are dependent on it. Through the name, the Seer (al-Baṣir) all the Divine ideas (al-A'yān T̲h̲ābitā) are discriminated. Through The Hearer (al-Samī) knowledge of the aptitudes of the essences of things is gained. Through the Determiner (al-Qadīr) omnipotence bestows existence generally on the essence. Through the 'one who wills' (murīd) omnipotence diverts its attention specially towards conferring existence on essences and revealing their aptitudes and 'Shakilāt'. The Speaker (al-Kalīm) addresses the essences of things with 'Be' (Kun) and they don the apparel of existence.

Just now I have used the word 'Divine ideas' or 'the Essences' of things [al-a'yān-al-t̲h̲ābita]. Now is the time to give it a little more consideration.

From eternity God Almighty is the Knower, has the attribute of knowledge. "The attribute of Knowledge in the Essence of God is eternal, was eternal and will be eternal". Knowledge is impossible without ideas, the Knower will have Knowledge of some 'Known' only. Therefore, in these three hypostases of God, viz., the Knower, the Known and Knowledge, distinction could be made from the beginning. Now what are Divine ideas? They are the essences of contigent beings, i.e. all things excepting God are created, God is their Creator. He creates the creatures after knowing them and does not know them only after creating them, otherwise it would necessarily imply a hiatus of ignorance in God's Knowledge, which is unthinkable. Created beings, which are known by God from eternity, or in other words, the ideas of God, or the essences of things, according to which things are created, are called al-A'yān-al-Thābitā—the essences of things. They are also termed 'ideas'', they are the determinations of the Divine Knowledge and are also called 'nonentities' and 'non-beings' because they are mere forms of knowledge, they do not have independent external existence; according to external existence they are, as it were, non-existent. They possess subsistence in knowledge, according to them only creation takes place in the external; they themselves subsist in the Knowledge of God *alone*, they never have any external existence. Therefore, Shaykh Akbar remarks : "The 'A'yān never even smelt the odour of existence."[48] They are indestructible, for their annihilation would mean the destruction of the Knowledge of God; they are eternal. Scholastic theologians have termed them 'the Known Unknown' (Ma' lūm-Ma'dūm). In the terminology of philosophers and thinkers they are called "Essences" and the Mu'tazilites speak of them technically as 'the subsistents' (Thābitāt).

According to the eminent Ṣūfīs, essences of things are not created by the creation of any creator—(ja'l-i-ja'il). What we have said before should make this statement intelligible. In one of the foregoing paragraphs I have explained why the essences of things are called "nonentities". They have no external existence; they subsist in knowledge alone. How could that be called 'Created' which does not have external existence at all. The same idea has been presented by Jāmī thus[49]:

The 'essences' never assume manifested
forms.
They certainly are not creations of any
creator.
Since creation is but an expression of
the light of Existence.
It is not meet to endow it with the
quality of not being."

Every essence has an individual aptitude of its own which is spoken of as ability or natural propensity. This is, as it were, the essential nature or characteristic by which it can be distinguished from other essences. On account of this characteristic every essence is a determinate form. Due to this determination it has its special aptitudes which are not exactly similar to any other essence; in this sense every essence has a limitation of its own. In the terminology of the Qur'ān this aptitude of essence has been spoken of as 'Shākilah' "Say, every one acts according to his own Shākilah (disposition or aptitude)."[50-51]

Essences of things are the mirror of the existence of God and the external world is the reflection which is revealing itself through this mirror. This reflection is also called the 'shadow' (Ẓil), because as shadow is revealed by light and when there is no light it would be non-existent, so also the world, too, is born out of the Existence of God and according to its own nature is not-being and darkness. Shaykh Akbar has got a clue from the following verse."[52]

"Hast thou not turned thy vision to thy Lord ?—How He doth prolong the Shadow."[53]

That is to say, thy Lord has spread the relative existence, which is a shadow of the real existence, on the essences of contingent things and thus the contingent things are in reality reflected entities which express outwardly the essences which subsist in the Knowledge of God.

The essences of things have been regarded as the mirror of God's existence. Now, note that one of the characteristics of a mirror is that the reflection of the mirror depends on its shape and design. If there is curvature in a mirror the reflection, too, will be curved, if the mirror is long the reflection, too, will be long and if the mirror is small the reflection also will be small, whereas the person whose image is reflected in the mirror remains quite unaltered. These various reflections are due to the shape or form of the mirror.

Another peculiarity of the mirror is that it is not visible by itself because you see your image in the mirror and not the mirror.

A third characteristic is that the mirror is not attributed with the image seen in the mirror. We do not say that the mirror alone is just the image or the image is the mirror itself, on the other hand the mirror is the cause or instrument of reflecting the image.

Now, note that the essences of things, or al-'A'yān thabitā, which are the ideas of God, resemble a mirror in which :—

1. The Being of God remaining in its own immutable state, as it ever was, manifests itself according to the aptitudes of the essences.

Essences are mirrors wherein
God reflects Himself."[54] (Jāmī)

As the person, who is standing before a mirror, remains quite unaltered and the length and the concavity of the mirror does not affect him in the least, on the other hand reveals all his aptitudes, so also God remaining immutable and maintaining His state and attributes reveals Himself without being affected with plurality and multiplicity through the attribute of light. Hence it is that the Divine Aspects (Being attributes etc.) come to be associated with the world of creation or phenomena.

2, 3. Essences are not visible in the outward world, they subsist in Divine Knowledge alone, have no external existence. The manifestation of their āthār (inherent effects) excites the suspicion that probably essences themselves have come into existence. The Existence of God Himself has revealed itself through the forms of these essences. Whatever defect or loss is appearing in existence, all of it pertains to the inner being of mirrors i.e. is an expression of the aptitudes of the essences. The author of Gulshan-i-Raz expresses it thus :[56]

Not-Being is the mirror of the Absolute
Being,
The Shining of "The Truth" is reflected in it
When Not-being is set opposite to Being
It catches its reflection in a moment.
That Unity is exposed to view in this
plurality,
Like as when you count one it becomes many.
Though all numbers have one for their
starting point,
Nevertheless you cannot come to the end
of them.

For as much as Not-being in itself is
pure,
Therein is reflected "the hidden treasure".
Read the tradition " I was a hidden
treasure"
That you may see clearly this concealed
mystery.[57]

Most of the eminent Ṣūfīs quote a holy tradition which has been cited by Ghazzālī and Shaykh Akbar, and men of spiritual discernment admit its authenticity—
It is as follows:[58]

"I was à hidden treasure, and I desired to become known and I created the world in order to be known."[59]

The Essence of God is a hidden treasure. In order to observe its beauty and perfection outwardly It adorned the mirrors of the essences and revealed Itself in those mirrors. The forms of things that subsisted in the Inward plane (in Wāḥidiyyat) were revealed in the Outward plane and in them It saw Itself and Its own works.

A gnostic has explained the holy Tradition in the following excellent couplets :[60]

"All that is, hath emerged under the stress of
love.[61]
It is through love alone what is non-existent
becomes existent.
The caprice of the Beloved is a reaction to
the constancy of the lover,
It has projected this world and disclosed all
its Secret !
It is in response to our constancy that the
caprice of the Beloved, is at play !
Herein lies the truth of "I desired."
In one sense He is the Beloved, in another,
He is the Lover Himself, if you know the
truth !"

The gist of whatever I have stated so far can be technically expressed in the following paragraph :

The Pure Essence, without consideration of any attribute, is the Absolute State of Abstract Unity (Aḥadiyyat) which has been referred to above as a 'Secret treasure'. The Absolute Essence according to the absolute knowledge of the Essence is Waḥdat and according to attributive knowledge Wāḥidiyyat. Waḥdat consists of brief observance and Wāḥidiyyat is comprised in detailed observance and from this point of view the Essence is independent of all other existences, as it is said:[62] "Lo, Allah is altogether Independent of (His) Creatures."[63] The Essence beholds its own Being, is independent of the manifestation of attributes and can do without the world.

The robe of Love is independent, free
From need to soil with dust its purity;
When Actor and Spectator are the same
What means this "we" and "thou" ? there
is no "we."[64-65]

The Ṣūfīs call it "Perfection of the Essence" (Kamāl-i-Dhātī). Aḥadiyyat, Waḥdat and Wāḥidiyyat are called the Divine ranks, these are the internal ranks of the Essence.

For revealing "the perfection of the names" (Kamāl-i-Asmāī God Almighty desired to observe His totality and detail in the external, just as they are observed in the internal stages, therefore, He made the world i.e. manifested Himself in the form of the essences of things. Here the details of the external mundane planes are presented which are a detailed description of the worlds of 'Soul', 'Similitudes' and 'Body', and the comprehensive stage of man. But I propose to delete them here, yet it would not be out of place to mention that it should not be considered that these external planes are not included in the Essence of God. Such is not the case. These words imply the individualisation of the Absolute Being. By actualisation of the potential the world is not excluded from the Essence of God and neither is a void created in it. The Essence remains the same as it was before. The Illumination of the Essence, due to which the shadow of existence falls on the essences of things is spoken of as the "Most Holy Emanation" (Faiḍh Aqdas). Illumination of the Names, (Tājalli-i-Asmāī), "The Divine Breath", (Nafs-i-Raḥmānī) in the terminology of the eminent Ṣūfīs. A summary of this statement can be expressed in the couplets of a gnostic thus:[66]

He has rendered the world into a mirror
wherein He shows Himself unto Himself.
All that is seen and unseen is but a reflection
of His Beauty !
When that Beauty desired to come in the
form of glory,
It put on the visage of this world of
time and space !
Whose is any name ? whose is any identity ?
Is there anything here and there other than He ?
He alone is there under every name and
under every identity.

Now the last couplet requires some explanation.

"God (Ḥaqq) is manifest in the form of actual things and things exist through the real existence of God (Ḥaqq)." The manifestation of that which appears in manifestation is of three kinds:

(1) The manifestation of the abstract in abstract, as the manifestation of the Essence of God in the multiple Divine Names.

(2) The manifestation of the abstract in matter, as the manifestation of the soul in the multiple parts of the body.

(3) The manifestation of matter in matter, as the manifestation of a single person in multi-coloured mirrors

In all the above three illustrations it cannot be conceived that mutability, division, 'fusion' or 'unity' is possible in the very nature of that which manifests itself. Shaykh Aḥmad Sarhindī in his Maktūb No. 89 Volume III writes:

"The meaning which I infer from "Everything is He" (Hamā Oost) according to the statements of the Ṣūfīs, is that all these diverse temporal pluralities are the manifestations of the One Essence which is Pure and Sublime. It could be illustrated thus. The form of Zaid manifests itself in different mirrors, here only one being of Zaid is manifested. There is not the slightest room for divisibility or union or fusion or mutability. In spite of all these the being of Zaid maintains its original state; due to these forms or images it has neither suffered nor gained anything. Where the being of Zaid is found, there is not the slightest trace of these forms to which divisibility or union or fusion could be related. The secret of 'He is now as He was before' should be sought here. For in the stage where God is, the phenomenal world, before its manifestation, had no room to exist. Even after manifestation there is no room for the phenomenal world. Consequently, one would have to admit that "Even now He is the same as He was before."

In brief the relation found between that which manifests itself (God) and the manifested (created things) is not that of fusion or union i. e. it does not necessarily follow that that which manifests is fused and united together with the manifested. Neither is it necessary that that which manifests itself may be divided in manifestation and suffer a change.

"The Beloved is ourselves but not by
virtue of "Union",[67]
The house of our being is filled with
Him but by means of no 'fusion',
In our faith wisdom is nothing but
gnosis.
Except this we admit no fundamentals
and no corollaries.

The relation found between the 'manifest' and the 'manifested', between the Lord and the 'abd, between God and the created beings, is quite different from all other relations. For the manifest in all its aspects is not the same as the manifested. Neither it is quite the other in all its aspects. Neither there is pure 'identity' nor pure 'otherness'. Think over this relation for a while:

1. Pure Otherness: If we regard the relation of otherness between Ḥaqq and K͟halq as literal and real and identity as suppositional and figurative, as is the creed of the creationists and has been offered by the scholastic theologians as well, we will then have to posit the same relation between Ḥaqq and K͟halq, as is found between a wooden cot and the carpenter or between a painting and the painter, and we will have to deny flatly that the very Essence of God encompasseth all things and nothing could exist without the omnipresence and companionship of God. In the preceding Chapter I have shown in detail that the relation of omnipresence and

companionship is posited and supported by the Prophet's Traditions and the Qur'ānic verses. To interpret encompassment and omnipresence and say that it is encompassment or omnipresence in knowledge only, would be overlooking the evident connotation of the clear verses of the Qur'ān. Such a belief according to Sharī'at is false, it is as it were indulging in false worship (Shirk) and consequently this belief will stand in the way of attaining the nearness of God:[68]

This vaunting of empty claims—how long ?
This assertion of thy being, thou fool,—how long ?
God exists and thou, too, doth exist,
Thou insensible ! This clash of self and
duality—how long ?

2. Pure Identity: This doctrine is just the opposite of the above. Here the relation of identity between Ḥaqq and Khalq is regarded as literal and real and otherness as hypothetical and suppositional. This is the creed of the atheists and the heretics. According to it the relation between Ḥaqq and Khalq is the same as is found between Zaid and his limbs, between wax and its different shapes or between a sea and its variegated waves. Ignorant pretenders to Ṣūfīsm and confirmed atheists quote several illustrations of this kind and consider them to be right in all their aspects. According to them the meaning of the words: "He that knows himself knows his Lord."[69] Is that such a man is himself God, the essences of both of them are one ; identity is not that of existence, it is one of the essences :[70]

In the ocean of life there is nothing
more precious than to know oneself,
We have, therefore, chosen to revolve
round ourselves like a whirl-pool !

If you reflect on the theory of the Six Descents presented in the foregoing paragraphs, you will come to know that pure identity is the result of certain ambiguities inherent in this theory. Due to mere lack of explanation these ambiguities lead the inadept to the conviction that according to existence and essence nothing could even be thought of except God. Further the statements of the experts which emphasise the identity of existence are believed by them to refer to the identity of essence only. Just reflect over the following quatrain of the eminent Jāmī.

In neighbour, friend, companion, Him we see,[71]
In beggar's rags or robes of royalty,
In Union's cell or in Distraction's haunts,
There is none but He—by God, there is
none but He.[72]

Swearing twice and emphasising on the oath the identity of existence is being announced. Apparently it could be understood also that existentially and essentially there is only one Being, there is not a vestige of otherness. Think over the following couplets of another gnostic :

Knowledge of Certainty has developed into
reality of Certainty,[73]
I have here just put it on record ;
All that is, is most certainly He Himself!
Life, life's love, sweet heart, heart
itself and its workings.

Seemingly, here too, the otherness of essence appears to be missing. In the following quatrain Jāmī has boldly denied the otherness of Essence.

Rase the words 'this' and 'that', duality
Denotes estrangement and repugnancy.[74]
In all this fair and faultless universe
Naught but one Substance and one Essence see.[75]

At another place he says clearly;[76]

What is there in the two worlds except
the Single Essence ?
Nothing exists in the entire Universe
except He !

It is evident that here only One Essence of God is posited and separate proofs of the essence of khalq and the Essence of Ḥaqq is not furnished.

Reflect on the mutual correlation between the Essence of God, Divine names, and the essences of things. You will be surprised if you go through the explanation of these realities in the treatises on the theory of Six Descents. Clear instruction in regard to the relation between the Essence of God and the essences of things has been utterly forsaken. Whatever is explained here summarily amounts to this much only that the realities of the essence of things are the Divine names; the essences of things are Divine ideas, they do not exist in the external world but subsist in the Divine Knowledge. When the Divine names are revealed in the essence of things, the external world makes its appearance.

Now there are two aspects of the external world or external essences (which are a reflection of the essence of things).

1. As a reality: By this is implied the manifestation of God in the forms of phenomenal objects. It is also called "Tajallī-i-Shuhūdī".

2. As a determination: According to this aspect things are called contingent and created and all imperfections and defects are attributed to them. A gnostic has expressed it thus:[77]

From the standpoint of 'form' things
seem other than God,
If you look into their inward aspect
all things are He!
The one is what has to vanish one day,
The other is what has to endure in eternity!

The words "The one is what has to vanish one day"[78] in the Qur'ānic verse refer to the Created things and the words "The other is what has to endure in eternity" refer to God Almighty.[79-80] Jāmī expresses the same idea thus:[81]

Whether one is inclined to evil or to good,
Whether one is an inmate of a cloister
or a monk in a monastery,
From the view point of 'form', everyone
is other than He,
But from the view point of reality everything is He and none other than He!

The 'Otherness' which is being caused by determination is called 'hypostatical Distinction" (Ghayriat-ī-I'tebārī). Gnostics—'Men of certitude'—have regarded this as 'real' and 'actual' and not hypothetical (Wahmī) or mere suppositional, because it is a mode of the Essence of God. The inexpert have regarded this as unreal and suppositional, thinking that if we regard it as the other, it is, if not, it has no reality. This is the creed of the atheists and the heretics. Ultimately the words "hypostatical otherness" were discarded and instead the words 'real' and 'technical' were employed. But if the gnostic had described the relationship between the Essence of God and the essences of things more explicitly, all these misunderstandings would have been removed and heresy and atheism would not have found their way among people.

In order to explain 'Otherness' explicitly, it is necessary to show clearly that the essences of things or al a'yān-al-thābitā subsist in the Mind of God, so in accordance with this subsistence identity is predicated from the beginning to eternity. But from the point of view of "essences" otherness is predicated from beginning to eternity. The essences of Created beings have form and have determination and limitation, whereas the Essence of God has no form, is unlimited, is Absolute and is free from all the essentials of form. The Essences of things subsist in Divine Knowledge, and do not possess their own independent existence. The Essence of God exists in Itself, is Self-Existent, depending on nothing else but Itself. The essences of Created beings possess non-existential attributes and the Essence of God is gifted with existential attributes i.e. it is attributed with life, knowledge, will, power, hearing, sight and speech. The essences of Created beings are passive. Having no existence and existential attributes of their own, they possess no activity of their own; whereas the Essence of God is active. In short, the Essence, of God is existent and the essence of the Created beings non-existent; therefore from the point of view of "essences" there is 'otherness' and from the point of view of 'existence' there is real identity, for the Existence of God is nothing but the existence of the Created beings themselves i. e. the Existence of the One God alone manifests itself in form of the essences of the created beings.

If the difference and distinction between the Essence of God and the essences of Created beings thus lucidly explained and is supported by Qur'ānic verses, the doctrine of pure identity is totally refuted, misunderstandings are removed and the true creed becomes obvious.

Why do we regard the doctrine of pure identity as atheism and heresy? It is because to deny the otherness of things means denying the Qur'ān. If there is no otherness between the Essence of God and the essences of Created beings between the Creator and the creatures and between the worshipper and the worshipped, why were the prophets sent? Why was the Law (Sharī'at) imposed? Who are being commanded to live a pious life and do good deeds? By presenting the same argument, the gnostic of Rūm is demonstrating two essences, viz., the essence of Ḥaqq and the essence of Khalq thus:[82]

> There is no way but one which leads
> to the Reality,
> Else the Mission of prophets will look
> futile,
> Since the prophets have come to forge
> bonds,
> What will they bind when there is but
> a single body?

At some other place he has expressed the otherness of the essences of phenomenal things more explicitly thus:[83]

> I am not of the Essence of God but an
> essence apart,
> I am just a manifestation of His Light.

2. If the 'Otherness' of the essence of the 'abd is denied, will the Essence of God alone, be regarded as the source of all evils and imperfections? Who will deserve Credit or Discredit? To whom would be ascribed wickedness, goodness, Islam and Unbelief and sins? Is it not clear heresy and atheism to regard the most Holy Being of God as the origin and source of all evils and imperfections? That is the reason why Jāmī distinguishes between the two essences i.e. the Essence of God and the essences of created beings and regards the Essence of God as free from all the aptitudes of the essence of the 'abd.

He is different from everything in
essence and attributes,[84]
'He is not in the likeness of anything' !

"To apply the names of "Allah" and "The Merciful" etc. to Created beings is sheer infidelity and heresy. Similarly to apply the names suitable to grades of created things to the Deity is the height of misconception and delusion.

O You who deem yourself infallible
In certitude a very oracle.[85]
Each grade of being has its proper name;
Mark this, or you will become an infidel.[86]

Some of the statements of Jāmī which I have cited above and which posited the existence of One Essence could be explained thus: Here Jāmī is speaking about the state of Aḥadiyyat. By Essence he means the Essence of God and by 'existence' the Self-existent Being of God Himself. It is evident that 'Existence is identical with the 'Essence' of God. He is looking neither at the relative existence nor at the essences of Created beings. This is the description of the stage when the gnostic passes away from what belongs to him and nothing remains in his vision save the One Reality. Therefore, except identity nothing is considered and observed. Hence, such statements are correct from the restricted point of view of the gnostic and actually they are not correct.

3. If no relation of otherness exists between the Essence of God and the essences of the Created beings, then the Essence of God becomes the source of all differences, oppositions and contradiction; for example, Zaid wants something and 'Umar something which is opposed to Zaid. As both of them are united together and are supposed to be a single part of the real Essence of God, so it is necessary that contradictions should gather in the Essence of the Absolute. Similarly, knowledge and ignorance, want and affluence, temporality and eternity, life and death, unbelief and Islam, joy and sorrow etc. which are the opposites of one another would be posited in the Essence of God and their presence there will be justified. This is self-evidently false and contrary to reason.

4. The Qur'ān posits the essence of the 'abd as the 'other' and regards the essence of the 'abd as a supplicant

a trustee, a vicegerent and as aint. Denying the essence of the 'abd is equivalent to refuting want and trust and vicegerency and saint-ship and the refutation of these Qur'ānic conceptions is clearly misguidance, unbelief, atheism and heresy.

The essence of the 'abd is purely a mendicant, existence does not originally belong to him, it has no existential attributes, it possesses no activity of its own; it is not vested with ownership and rulership. Huwiyya and Anniya, attributes and actions, and ownership and sovereignty are found in it as a trust. He is a trustee. When he employs the Divine trust versus the universe he is called the vicegerent of God and when he uses it in relation to God he becomes a saint. These only are the pure aspects of the 'abd, viz. want trust, vicegerency and saintship. Now he should endeavour to efface himself in the Essence of God on which depends his perfection. When in this state of effacement and absorption the 'abd passes away God alone remains! At that moment it is said that there is neither Creator nor the Creatures, neither the Knower nor the Known, neither the Seeker nor the one sought and neither the Lover nor beloved. This is the stage of "total passing-away", it is complete effacement, is a "retrocession cf trust."—

> "Perfect poverty is God indeed"[87-88]
> Love, the lover and the loved here
>   are but one,[89]
> When the question of union does not arise,
>   why talk of any state of separation ?

In no stage could 'abdiyat be dispensed with, and the role of devotion avoided. So long one lives and retains reasoning and senses it is his duty to observe the Law (Shari'-at), it is compulsory for him to do so. An 'abd is 'abd and the Lord, Lord ! A reversal of the reality is impossible. The way of prophets and the practice of saints are witnesses to the fact that the commandments to servants are never annulled, the words "And serve thy Lord till the inevitable (i.e. death) cometh unto thee"[90-91] refer to the same fact. But 'abdiyat alone is the cause of freedom—what is Freedom ?

"It is but to cut oneself off absolutely from everything other than God."[92]

True freedom is enjoyed by the man, who after freeing his mind from the affairs of this world and the next establishes a relation of 'abdiyat with God. Freedom means this humility and obedience—freedom cannot be gained without obedience:

"Only the bondsmen are really free"[93] (Ḥāfiz)
How aptly it has been said:[94]
Lordliness is lordly through service alone,
Service indeed is the perfect form of Lordliness!
From the time I came under your bondage
I have felt a freeman!
The moment I became your prisoner I
felt I was a king!

Only after becoming an 'abd man gains the positions of the trustee of God, the vicegerent of God and the saint of God. Such an 'abd can say "I am thy 'abd"[95] and later: "He that has seen me has seen Allah."[96-97]

In short it is necessary to distinguish between the essence of the Created beings and the Essence of God, between the Lord and the 'abd and between things and Existence. The man who would not make this distinction is ill-mannered, is an atheist, a heretic; he is not wise, he is unwary. There is a difference between Existence and things. Things are just the mirrors of the manifestation of Existence. Therefore, as essences things are definitely other than God and Existence in its real aspect is definitely God Himself. Waḥdatu'l-Wujūd or Unity of Being is in view of Existence and not in view of things. Pure identity is sheer heresy and atheism which denies the essential otherness of things. According to the aspect of thing "Everything is from Him", is quite true, and according to existence "Everything is He" is definitely justifiable.

CHAPTER V

SELF-DETERMINISM

Disciple: O, ye who have shared the
ecstasy of the elect of the
field of Badr:
The problem of free will and determinism baffles my mind.
Preceptor: The wings of the falcon swing
to the hand of the Sultan,
The wings of the crow drive but to the
graveyard ! (Iqbāl)

No problem has been more persistent in Philosophy than the question of Free will and Determinism. In spite of the theoretical character of the problem man has been enthusiastically engaged with it for centuries. For, after all, the Issue is not only one of merely academic import. Our systems of theology, politics, economics, education and criminology are based upon the primary ways in which man has met this historic query.

If we are not free moral agents, let theology explain to us why should we be doomed to Hell. Let criminology show us the significance of punishing a thief. And why does Ethics insist on purifying the heart and improving the morals ? If we are free, why do we, then, not, according to Spinoza, seem to have control even on our own tongue ? Why is the storm of passion overpowering for man, and why reason has always been a slave to passions ? "An angry child believes that it freely desires vengeance, a timid child believes that it freely desires to run away; further, a drunken man believes that he utters from the decision of his mind words, which when he is sober, he would willingly have withheld; thus, too, a delerious man, a garrulous woman, a child and others of like complexion, believe that they speak from the free decision of their mind, when they are in reality unable to restrain their impulse to talk."[1] Our consciousness of Freedom", says Spinoza, "is a subjective illusion arising from the fact that men are conscious of their own actions and ignorant of the causes by which they are conditioned."[2]

To my mind reflective thought has not been able to unravel the difficulties of this old problem, to offer a satisfactory solution of it. It is still a "problem"—perhaps a puzzle ! Realising that the intellect was unable to solve it the Prophet of Islam said:[3]

"Maintain silence when people talk about predestination"—This command was addressed to the common people, the gnostic was told:[4]

"Do not discuss predestination because it is a secret of God and such a secret should not be disclosed." The latter assertion shows that Islam has revealed this important secret to those who have the capability of understanding it—about whom has been said:[5]

"Verily in this is a Message for anyone that has a heart and understanding or who gives ear and earnestly witnesses (the truth[6]).

The greatest Muslim Ṣūfī and Philosopher, S͟hayk͟h Muḥyidin Akbar is of the same opinion. Says he:[7]

"The secret of predestination is the greatest of all sciences and God Almighty reveals it to only those whom He has particularly selected for complete gnosis."

At the outset, just cast a glance at the doctrine of Determinism. Whosoever believes in God cannot but help in admitting Him as the Creator of all his actions. Even as God is the Creator of our bodies and souls, so is He the Creator of our acts too. This doctrine is strictly in accordance with the teachings of the Holy Qur'ān. It is expressly stated in the Qur'ān:[8]

"Verily all things have been created by decree and everything they do is in the books."[9] Now, "things" include "acts" also and God being "Creator of everything"[10]—it necessarily follows that He is the Creator of acts too. If acts had not been created, God would have been the Creator of certain things but not of all, and then His words, "Creator of everything"[10] would be wrong—far exalted is God above that.

We do not need this deductive argument even. It is clearly stated in the Qur'ān:[11] "God has created you and what ye make." This makes God the Creator of all our actions.

This is the positive statement of the matter. There is no ambiguity or vagueness in it. Think a little over the negative statements.

Negatively God denies that there is any Creator other than Himself when He says:[12]

"Or have they made associates with God who can create as He creates so that the creation seems familiar to them? Say, God is the Creator of everything and He is the One, the Dominant." (S. XIII,16)

Now suppose God has created man and man creates his own actions. It is certain that acts are more numerous than men themselves, for each man creates innumerable acts. It follows that the creation of man—the creature of God—is greater than the creation of God, the Creator of man. This is palpably nonsense. The creature cannot be more powerful than the Creator. Therefore God creates not man alone but his actions also.[13] "God is the only Creator, the Agent, the Doer." The whole universe is created by Him, man and his acts are all included in the Universe, therefore, all these are His "Creatures".

In the Jāvāid Nāmā, Iqbal expresses the same 'unity in effects' and 'unity in acts' thus:[14]

Do ye know who gives the talent to perceive?
How does the houri emerge from the dust?
Wherefrom comes the philosophers' power to think?
Wherefrom comes the speakers' power to speak?
Wherefrom comes the heart and wherefrom that
which sways it?
Wherefrom the common place and wherefrom the
wonder-fraught?
The warmth of thy speech is not thine!
The flame of thy action is not thine!
These gifts spring from Nature's bounty
Nature, in turn, is from nature's Sustainer!

This thesis is supported by the spoken words of the Prophet of Islam. It is said that 'Umar asked the Prophet[15]—"What thinkest thou of that in which we are engaged ? Is it upon a matter which is already completed or a matter only now begun !" The Prophet replied. "Upon a matter already completed". 'Umar said, "Then shall we not have trust (i.e. why should we endeavour to do anything when the whole thing is fixed and completed)". The Prophet answered, "Perform (what ye are about) for everyone is prepared for that for which he is created". 'Umar said[16] : "Now to work is good" and busied himself in his work. So nobody can sit idle, pleading predestination in support of his argument. Performance of duty now becomes a pleasure, effort is freed from anxiety. We realise that the work is facilitated for every person for which he is born.

On another occasion people asked the Prophet of Islam :[17] "What thinkest man of the spells and charms which we employ and the drugs wherewith we treat ourselves ? Do these reverse the decree of God ! " He replied, "These come of the decree of God." The following statement of his is clearer and more lucid :[18]

"Truly no man believes until he believes in God and in the decrees of God, be it for good or ill."

The teachings of Islam have made this aspect of Determinism quite clear, and it explains to us only this much, that God is the Creator of everything. But the whole of the teaching of Determinism does not conflict with free-will or Indeterminism. Apparently this seems to be a strange thesis, combining two irreconcilables—Predestination and Free-will. I hasten to marshal my arguments in support of what I have said. First, let me formulate the thesis of freedom of will and the responsibility as stated in the Qur'ān.

Together with the assertion : "That creation is from God"[19] man is held responsible for his actions. He is accredited with acts and "Merits",[20] in a true sense, for which he is rewarded and punished, and on account of which God issued commands and prohibitions, and announced promises and threats. Says the Qur'ān in lucid terms[21] : "On no soul doth

God place a burden greater than it can bear. It gets every good that it earns and it suffers every ill that it earns" (S. II, 286).

Here the responsibility of action is placed upon man. He earns his good and suffers for his evil. It is obvious, that there cannot be a true moral act, if the individual, who performs it, is not responsible for its execution. A person asleep or under an anaesthetic, a very young child, an idiot, and one under hypnosis, are not moral agents, because they do not act on the basis of rational will and choice. And when the Qur'ān says:[22] "If ye did well, ye did well for yourselves, if ye did evil (ye did it) against yourselves,"—it is then holding man clearly responsible for his actions, on the basis of rational will and free choice. The same has been expressed by Hasan Ibn-'Ali thus:[23] "God is not obeyed through compulsion, nor is He disobeyed by reason of an overwhelming force. He has not left His servants entirely without work to do in His Kingdom." "Let here be no compulsion in religion"[24] is the mandate of the Qur'ān. If there is compulsion in the execution of an act, it cannot be termed an ethical action. Sāhl Bin 'Abdullā remarks[25]—"God did not strengthen the pious through compulsion. He strengthened them through faith." One of the greatest Ṣūfīs has laid down the law when he said, "Whoever believes not entirely in predestination is an infidel[26] and whoever says that it is impossible to disobey God is a sinner."[27] To disobey God, man must be attributed with free choice. It is possible to disobey God, therefore, man has free choice which he exercises whenever he sins.

Iqbāl presents this choice, freedom of will and power, enthusiastically in the following couplets:[29]

Do not enchain thy feet with Fate
There is always a way out under this moving dome.
If thou believest me not, get up and find out,
Once the chains are thrown off, the path will
    reveal itself for thee !

In his Jāwaid Nāmā he strikes a new note thus:[30]

The denizens of the earth have bartered theirself,
They have not caught the secret of Destiny,

Destiny's secret lies concealed in a single word.
Destiny changes with every change in you
Shouldst thou turn into dust the wind will
carry you away,
If, into a stone, thou canst hurl yourself against
glasses !
If, into a dew, you will cling to earth,
If, into an ocean, you will have life ever-
lasting !

Now we have before us, both the thesis and anti-thesis clearly stated. Man is determined in his action. God creates man and man's action as well—Thesis. Man is free in his choice and therefore responsible for his actions for which he is rewarded and punished—Anti-thesis.

To remove this contradiction I would ask you to indulge in mental abstraction for a while. According to Hegel, thinking is as difficult for a weak mind as it is difficult for a weak-back to carry a heavy load. Both are helpless—neither the one can do consistent and persistent thinking, nor the other carry a heavy weight.

How do the Ṣūfīs reconcile these contradictions. By a higher synthesis. Here a clear knowledge of the metaphysical background of the problem is necessary. We know the Ṣūfīs believe that God exists and that He is the Absolute Knower. Knowing implies knowledge and the object known. These three phases of God could be clearly distinguished from the very beginning. He knows His own thoughts, these being the object of His knowledge. Knowledge without the known is as impossible as is will without the objects willed, as is hearing without the things heard, and sight without the things seen. As God is the Knower since eternity, and as knowledge is impossible without the known, therefore, His objects of knowledge too are eternal i.e. they are uncreated. Knowledge is an attribute of God and cannot, therefore, be separated from Him, otherwise, ignorance will be ascribed to God. Since God is eternal and uncreated His knowledge also is uncreated; similarly, as his knowledge is perfect His ideas, too, would be perfect.

Now the ideas of God are technically called "Essences" by the Philosophers and the Ṣufīs call them[31] 'al'Ayan-al thābitā, the Fixed Prototypes or the latent realities. The essences are firstly uncreated and secondly perfect and immutable. It is evident that every essence will have its own characteristic or essential nature. In other words this is called the 'aptitude' of an essence, or in Qur'ānic Terminology, 'Shākila'.[32]

It should be carefully noted that as essences are uncreated and unchangeable, so their aptitudes and 'Shakilat', too, are immutable and uncreated. Jāmī says:[33] "Aptitudes are not created. The Creator does not create a thing against its innate aptitudes."

To understand the "Secret of Predestination", it would suffice to admit these few propositions, after fully grasping their import. The gist of all of them is that God exists from eternity. He is the Knower from eternity, that is, He is eternally attributed with knowledge. And for knowledge the known is necessary, therefore, the ideas of God are eternal, too, and uncreated. The ideas are called the 'essences' of things or Ayān' or contingent beings. When the ideas are eternal, then, all their aptitudes also will be eternal.

Now creation is an act of will. The will of God obeys the knowledge of God. Creation is nothing but the external manifestation or actualisation of the ideas of God or the "Essences". That which is manifested or actualised, exists internally in the mind of God, as an idea. Ideas actualised are called things; things are known internally and created externally. As they are finite or limited they are 'other' than the Being of God; the Being of God is free from all determinations and limitations.[34] "There is nothing whatever like unto Him, and He is the one that hears and sees (all things)."[35]

Now in the light of these truths consider the question of Determinism and Indeterminism. God is creating things, but they are being created according to their aptitudes. The aptitudes of the things themselves are not created by the Creator. They are uncreated and eternal. A fatalist cannot grasp this delicate point. He regards his 'essence' also as created. He thinks that his aptitudes, too, are created, whereas, they are eternal, as they are Divine ideas. If they are not eternal and are created by the Creator they would, then, have been necessarily negative before being created. A thing which is negative would always be negative, it cannot be positive, otherwise 'transformation of essence' will result, and this is impossible. If a fatalist comprehends this point he will not say, why my nature is made thus. Nature, which we are technically speaking of as the 'essence,' or 'ayn' was not made, it is not at all created and all its aptitudes are not created by the Creator, and it is, thus, free according to its real aptitude. But God is revealing these aptitudes and characteristics externally. He is bestowing existence on them—Creation is always the act of God.[36]

All that is stated above could be tersely expressed in a sentence. This is the Mystery of Predestination.[37]

"It is not possible for an 'ayn' to be manifested externally as far as its essence or attribute or action is concerned, except in accordance with its aptitude."[38]

Here both Determinism and Indeterminism are being reconciled. The essences of things which are the ideas of God (and God is their Knower) are manifesting themselves according to their aptitudes, peculiarities and characteristics. This is the aspect of choice and free-will, but God alone is manifesting them—this is the aspect of Determinism.

Movement is one but its relations are two-fold.

One relation is towards God, this is the relation of creation. All the acts are being created by God, He alone is the real Doer. Created things possess neither movement nor power.[39]

Another relation is posited towards created things, which is that of 'acquisition' i.e. actions are being created exactly according to the essential nature of things. In other words, whatever there is in the essence is being manifested through the agency of the Creator. When all the incidents are happening according to my aptitude, and nothing is imposed on me against my nature, I am, then free in the true sense of the word. That is why Shaykh Akbar says:[40] "Whatever has been definitely determined about us is in conformity with our nature, further we ourselves are determining it according to our aptitude." This tallies verbatim with the commandment of the Holy Qur'ān[41]—"And He giveth you of all that ye ask for."[42]

At another place it is stated more explicitly,[43] "Lo ! we shall pay them their whole due unabated."[44] "For God's is the final argument."[45] "The author of Gulshan-e-Raz makes God say:[46]

> The good and evil in thee,
> Owe their being from thine own nature ('ayn),
> It is my grace that gives a form
> To what is implicit therein.

The essence of every person is, as it were, a book in which are recorded all his real aptitudes and characteristics. God is creating things exactly in accordance with it. The eminent Jāmī has expressed it beautifully thus:[47]

> Thy Nature is but a copy of the 'Original Book,'
> It discloses what that there is in the Book of Eternal
> Secrets.
> Since it contained all preordained decrees,
> God has but acted in accordance therewith.

It would become more explicit if it is expressed technically, and the whole problem will thus be simplified. Essences or essential natures ('Ayan) are all the ideas of God and the decree of God will obey His ideas. Says Jāmī:[48]

> God is the Knower and the essences the Known.
> The Known thus becomes the dictator and the Knower
> the dictated.
> In accordance with the demand of the Known action
> follows.
> If it demands pain, pain is measured out, if grace
> grace is given.

Thus the decree of predestination applies to essential natures ('Ayān) i. e. the creation of God is in accordance with the aptitudes of Essences. That is why it is asserted "You are the Destiny" and "It is for you to decree."

Now after knowing this secret, we feel calm and contented and our relations from others are severed. We regard our own being as the source of good and evil, and the meaning of the saying "Whatever has befallen on us is the outcome of our own acts and attributes", becomes clear to us. Neither do we regard God as a tyrant, nor do we blame and deprecate our-fellow-beings, or speak ill of the environment. On the contrary, we take the responsibility on our own shoulders and addressing our own self, say:[49] "Thine hands only have earned, and thy mouth only has blown."[50] True it is: "Whatever of misfortune striketh you, it is what your right hands have earned."[51-52]

This reconciliation between Determinism and Indeterminism is found in the works of Iqbāl too, but his style is different and the technical terms used dissimilar. Further the contradiction is presented with such force, and the explanation offered with such brevity that contradiction is apparently visible but all the traces of reconciliation vanish. In his philosophical work—Reconstruction—we come across a few of such passages, that had Iqbāl explained them in more detail they would have been easier for us to understand. However, Iqbāl does offer a correct solution, though briefly. I shall dilate here on this brief statement. Explaining "Destiny" in the above mentioned book, Iqbāl says: "God created all things and assigned to each its destiny."[53] The destiny of a thing, then, is not an unrelenting fate working from without like a task-master, it is the *inward reach of a thing, its realisable possibilities which lie within the depths of its nature serially actualize themselves without any feeling of external compulsion.*

If we reflect on this one passage only, it would be clear that Iqbāl is giving free choice to the aptitudes of things, or in his own words, to 'the realizable possibilities' only. It would mean that aptitudes alone are manifesting themselves (by the agency of God) in the external world, so no compulsion is exercised on the being of thing, and in this sense the thing itself is Divine destiny. S͟hayk͟h Akbar had expressed the same idea thus:[54] "God bestows on a thing that which its essential nature demands." Iqbāl presents the same view differently:[55]

Raise thyself to such heights that before every fate befalls,
God shall ask you to say, what do you propose
to ordain for yourself?

Man is not determined in the sense that his aptitudes also may be regarded as Divine Creation. A man's essential nature, or in other words his essence ('Ayn) is uncreated and for the same reason he enjoys free-will and choice. Iqbāl is probably expressing the same idea in his words thus:[56]

'He still retains fate-destroying power,
Whom the ignorant call-but a victim of Fate!'

As Iqbāl honestly and sincerely admits the absolute power and profoundest wisdom of God Almighty, the explanation that I have given of the above couplet seems to be the only true explanation.

Together with this meaning of free-will and choice, remember also the meaning of the doctrine: "Everything comes from Him" as understood by Iqbāl. He has attributed God with the power of creation. If you note the above, you will be able to understand the reconciliation of this contradiction expressed in two sentences.[57] "Creation is from God and acquisition from contingent beings." The same sense is conveyed by the famous saying ascribed to Imām Ja'far-i-Sādiq: "Here there is neither Daterminism nor Indeterminism—the matter lies midway between the two."

Jāmi has expressed the same truth thus:[59]

Mark well this subtle point, each quality,
Each action that in substances we see,
On one side is attributed to us,
On one to "Truth", the sole Reality.[60]

If you have understood this "Mystery of Predestination" you will, then, also understand why 'the Perfect', the God-conscious feel a kind of calm and strength when by Predestination they imply 'Creation by God' and why the Ignorant being perplexed make no distinction between the prohibited and the permitted and regard Determinism as a privation of freedom. Iqbāl borrows a couplet from the poem of Qāzi Maḥmud Behri and in his Dialogues makes his "Pir" (Preceptor,) say:[61]

Fate serves as wings for the God-conscious,
The same Fate works as prison-house for the
Ignorant,
The wings of the falcon swing on to the
hand of the Sultan.
The wings of the crow drive but to the graveyard !

CHAPTER VI

GOOD AND EVIL

All good and all perfection that you see
Are of the "Truth" which from all stain is free;[1]
Evil and pain result from some defect,
Some lack of normal-receptivity.[2]
Wherever Being's ambit doth extend,[3]
Good and nought else but good is found, O friend,
All evil comes from "not-being", to wit,
From "other" and on "other" must depend.

Who can deny the existence of evil in the world? Is there anyone who is not undergoing pain and sorrow? Who did not physically or mentally fall a victim to some calamity? Breathes there anyone who does not complain of the woes inflicted on him by fate. Rest can only be enjoyed in the bowels of earth, nobody is destined to live a happy life on the face of the earth. Pain and sorrow, are called 'physical evils', by the philosopher, and certainly none can deny their existence. Similarly the depredations of ethical evil are known to all: Are not assassination, plunder, fornication, drinking, gambling, adultery, bribery and corruption rampant in every community? If the agony caused by these be converted into the form of smoke, darkness would pervade all over the world, and in this darkness such stifling anguish would be produced as would make even breathing impossible! Being continually worried by a host of physical and ethical evils man is forced to exclaim involuntarily:[4]

Were it in my power, I would have avoided
  to come in,
And were it in my power, I would have left
  it long ago!
Better would it have been had I not come
  on this desolate tavern,
Nor stayed, nor gone out!

Well, why is there so much evil in this world ? Why does so much tyranny, so many sins and offences and so much ugliness and wickedness exist ? Both for philosophers as well as divines, the problem of evil is the most delicate and most abstruse one. No other problem in the whole of the wide range of human experience is more perplexing than this. It is undoubtedly an enigma, which the sages and philosophers are unable to solve. Particularly those systems of thought which are established on a theological or teleological basis try to solve this problem but on being frustrated in achieving their end they exclaim :

> There was a Door to which I found no key,
> There was a veil Past which I could not see
> Some little Talk a while of Me and Thee,
> There seemed—and then no more of thee and Me ![6]

Why is this a riddle at all ! It is a riddle, because, if you admit that God is the Source or Origin of the Universe, then you will have to admit, too, that He is All-wise, All-powerful and All-good. Now when He is All-good, how could He be the Creator of evil ! How could the act of the All-wise be unwise ! Is there anything which could induce the Omnipotent to create evil ? So, if you deny the very existence of evil, and regard it as a mere illusion, you will after a little thinking find that error or illusion itself is an evil. How would you explain it ? And how would you be able to deny evil ? Grief and pain are real, even a plethora of words cannot change their reality. If you feel pain, then surely pain exists, because pain consists in the feeling; to say it is good is akin to saying black is white. God may regard it as anything else, but for us it is pain. Further will it be good for a person to tell him that God does not regard it as an evil, when he is broken down with pain ! The locus of pain is consciousness, if pain is found in consciousness how could pain be denied ! It would be a flowery expression if we call it illusion. But as a rose would be a rose irrespective of the name given to it, and will smell sweet, similarly you may give any name you like to pain, but it would remain. By substituting the name you cannot change its innate nature. However, while admitting God as All-powerful and All-good we cannot at the same time admit that evil exists, and neither does the denial of the existence of evil seem probable. How strange it is !

To avoid this paradox, some philosophers admit that God is good, but deny that He is Omnipotent. They think that if it is admitted that God is Omnipotent, He must ultimately be regarded responsible for the happening of every event. Further, since evil exists, it would naturally be said that it is being manifested by the Divine will. Unless it is proved that evil is not evil—and this is a contradiction in terms—it would have to be admitted that God tolerates the presence of evil ! It would not suffice to say that God tolerates these evils with a view to saving the world from a greater evil, or that He desires that it might not be deprived of the present joys. For, if He is Omnipotent, He can eradicate these other evils too, and without them also can benefit the world by these joys ! But God, who in spite of the fact that He can free the world from evil, tolerates evil could not be regarded as a good being. He could not be considered worthy of worship and the sacred appellation, 'God', could not be applied to Him. In view of the above it would be more satisfying for both, reason and the heart, to admit God as good, and together with it, be convinced of the fact that He does not possess power to remove evil from the world. He has powers for the acquisition of every individual good, but is powerless in the matter of the confirmation of collective good ! Such a being, considering his power, will and determination, when compared with another living being, may be termed Omnipotent particularly, if it is regarded as powerful enough to root out evil. When the faithful speak of the Absolute Power of God, they probably mean that evil will eventually suffer a defeat and good will triumph. But according to the literal meaning of the word, God cannot be regarded as Omnipotent, for He could not be regarded as 'Good' because He cannot either make a better world or does not want to make one. It is better to accept the first view.

John Stuart Mill has aptly expressed this theory. We would not commit ourselves to an unbelief if we copy it verbatim. He states as follows :—

"The only admissible moral theory of creation is that the Principle of Good *cannot* at once and altogether subdue the powers of evil, either physical or moral; could not place mankind in a world free from the necessity of an incessant struggle with the maleficent powers, or make them always victorious in that struggle, but could and did make them capable of carrying on the fight with vigour and with progressively increasing success. Of all the religious explanations of the order of nature, this alone is neither contradictory to itself nor to the facts for which it attempts to account. According to it, man's duty would consist, not in simply taking care of his own interests by obeying irresistible power, but in standing forward a not ineffectual auxiliary to a Being of perfect baneficence; a faith which seems much better adapted for nerving him to exertion than a vague and inconsistent reliance on an Author of Good who is supposed to be the author of evil. And I venture to assert that such has really been, though often unconsciously, the faith of all who have drawn strength and support of any worthy kind from trust in a superintending providence. There is no subject on which men's practical belief is more incorrectly indicated by the words they use to express it than religion. Many have derived a base confidence from imagining themselves to be favourites of an omnipotent but capricious and despotic Deity. But those who have been strengthened in goodness by relying on the sympathetic support of a powerful and good Governor of the world have, I am satisfied, never really believed that Governor to be, in the strict sense of the term, omnipotent. They have always saved his goodness at the expense of his power. They have believed, perhaps that he could, if he willed, remove all the thorns from their individual path, but not without causing greater harm to some one else, or frustrating some purpose of greater importance to the general well-being."[7]

The supporters of this theory state that this is accepted as true, then, there is no need for denying the existence of evil, or admitting God, All-good God, as the Creator of evil. Admitting the existence of evil we need neither try to prove it justifiable, nor do we need to devise excuses in regard to the wickedness of the world. We need not connive at evil, we detest evil, as God Himself detests it. We fight it as God is fighting it. We become a zealous member of God's party and help Him Who wishes us success and victory. No question of evil and good now remains to be settled. If there remains at all any question of evil it is —how should we quickly get rid of evil ? How should we bear it calmly and patiently ? And how should its weight be taken off the shoulder of the coming generations ?

This attempt at explaining evil regards God as 'finite' and evil in the universe, like good, as ultimate. Logically it is totally defective, neither can it furnish a correct solution of those moral problems as an explanation of which it has been offered.

First think over it for a while from the view-point of religion. The essence of religion consists in the belief that God alone is worthy of worship; assistance should be sought from Him alone. Prayer means humility and subjection. We express our humility before our Lord, who is our Master, our Helper, our Ruler and our Creator. He stands by us in all our difficulties and helps us in overcoming all our woes. Unless He is omnipotent He cannot help us. After seeking His shelter, we ought to enjoy peace and contentment, and this peace and contentment can be had only when we invest Him with absolute power. The God who Himself is fighting evil, who is not gifted with the strength to over-power it, who needs the assistance of man, who Himself is not safe from calamities and scourges, is Himself a pauper. How could he support me ? How can he be regarded as my Master and my Lord ? How can I worship such a God ? How can I express humility before him ? How can I join my hands in supplication before him ?

And when evil itself is an eternal reality, is a metaphysical principle, on what logical basis then could it be supposed that the united effort of man and God would be able to annihilate it ultimately ? When good is being resisted by an equal force, which is self-existing and permanent, how then it could be taken for granted that ultimately the state of the world would improve ? If evil is a thing found outside the spiritual world of God, then it would have to be admitted as an ineradicable resistance. If it is not a thing to be found existing outside, the possibility of evil and its incidence ought to be made an indispensable means of the realisation of good. If there is any real possibility of this world of ours being improved—it would be possible only when the universe is regarded as "good in the making."

Both Faith and Reason seem to be antagonistic to the attempt made by Mill and his followers in regard to the explanation of the existence of evil. How could faith regard God as limited and restricted, and after regarding Him as such pray to Him ? How can it regard evil as an independent and abiding source of the universe and thus admit association of another with God as co-equal ? How can we, then, explain evil ? Of course iss existence could not be denied, neither can the doctrine of God being the Absolute power, Absolute wisdom and Absolute good, be dispensed with, from a theological point of view ? The system of Philosophy which acknowledges these doctrines of faith, which admits the existence of God and regards Him as Absolute power and Absolute good cannot explain evil. How can the above system avoid those paradoxes which led some philosophers to regard the power of God as limited.

Sages admit the fact that no perfect solution of the problem of evil has been reached uptil now. As Avicenna puts it:[8]

> The secrets of Existence look hazy and
> are but partially revealed,
> The best of pearl scarcely shows its
> threadhole,
> Everyone has but surmised,
> The thing that matters remains still
> unsaid.

The limited intelligence of human beings could not so far grasp the full meaning and connotation of good and evil ! The Ṣūfīs of Islam too have explained evil, hints have been taken from the Holy Qu'rān, reason supports it. When compared with the explanation offered by other philosophers, this attempt of their's seems to us original and vigorous. God has been admitted as the Creator of good and evil, yet evil has not been ascribed to God. Apparently this statement appears to be self-contradictory; however you should learn this art of 'commingling of contradictories' from the Ṣūfīs of Islam and remember:[9]

Affirmation and denial are at times both valid,
When aspects alter, relationships vary !

Before explaining evil it is necessary to dilate on some metaphysical premises of this theory.

According to the Ṣūfīs, the solution of all problems, can be had in the simple words of knowledge, the Knower and the known. They hold that God Almighty is the Knower, knowledge belongs to Him alone in reality and in itself; the essences of created beings are all His objects 'known', ideas.

The Qu'rān confirms and supports this doctrine. Besides, the person who believes in the existence of the Supreme Being will not regard his God as ignorant. The attribute of knowledge is in reality peculiar to God Almighty alone; it is solely ascribed to Him alone. Says the Qu'rān:[10] "It is He Who has knowledge and power."[11]

Now for knowledge one must necessarily have objects known. Knowledge is of course the knowing of an object or any known thing; without the 'known', knowledge is utterly impossible. Since God Almighty is the Knower since eternity (i.e. the attribute of knowledge is inseparable from the Being of God), the Being of God is eternal, so knowledge, too is eternal, otherwise it would imply that God is ignorant (and God is free from ignorance) and knowledge without object known is impossible; therefore, it follows, that the things known to Him, too, are eternal. God creates things with knowledge, says the Qu'rān:[12] "Should He know not what He created? And He is the Subtle, the Aware"[13] and knows them after creation too. The thing created is known by God.[14] "For He is the Knower of every creation."[15] Therefore, it is proved, that everything is essentially a known object and from eternity subsists in the Divine knowledge. In the terminology of the Ṣūfīs, the created things which are, from eternity, objects of God's knowledge are called the 'Essences of things,' ('Ayāni Th-ābitā). They are also termed the "Ideas of God". These are truly speaking, the modes or determinations of the Divine knowledge. They are also termed as 'non-entities' or 'Ādām or Mā'dumāt-i-Haqq' as they are the forms of knowledge and do not possess external independent existence. The philosophers and sages have preferred to call them as 'Essences' or quiddities' (Māhiyāt).

Now, concentrate your mind for a while on these "Essences". The Ṣūfīs regard them as 'other' than God. The Essence of God and the essences of the created things, are totally the 'Other' of one another. The Qu'rān implies their "Otherness" when it asks:[16] "Then will you fear other than God."[17] According to reason, too, it is clear, that the essences are 'other' than the Being of God. Note that they have been spoken of as "non-entities" or Mā'dumāt. They are 'relative' non-entities and not 'real' non-entities. Why are they spoken of as 'relative' non-entity? Because they do not have a permanent being of their own. God alone is self-existent.[18] In their birth and subsistence all the creatures owe their being to God alone. The 'essences' of created beings, by virtue of their origin and essential nature, are ideas in the mind of God, that is why they subsist in God's knowledge. As they do not possess being of their own they are called 'non-entities' ('Ādām).

When they do not have 'being' of their own, it is clear, they do not possess real 'attributes' of their own. In God Almighty, real being is His own, consequently, He possesses existential attributes, too, viz., Life[19] Knowledge,[20] Power,[21] Will,[22] Hearing,[23] Sight,[24] and Speech[25] and all of these have no existence in the essences of the created beings. Non-existent essences of created beings are not alive, and when such is the case, their real attribute would be 'death'. If they do not possess knowledge their attribute would be 'ignorance', if they do not have will, their attribute would be will-lessness (Iḍṭirār), if they are not vested with power, their attribute would be powerlessness ('Ijz), and if they are not gifted with the sense of hearing, sight and speech they would be blind, deaf and mute. The Ṣūfīs call them "Non-existential" attributes, and according to them the absence of existential attributes is synonymous with the presence of non-existential attributes.

When the essences of the created beings are devoid of being and attributes, how can, action be ascribed to them. Actions are committed through attributes and attributes subsist in being or existence. When the attributes of existence are negatived actions too are negatived

How can effects (Athār) be produced by a being that is devoid and deprived of attributes and actions and subsists in knowledge alone ? Thus, the essences of created being are totally deprived of being, attributes, actions and effects.

In short, since the essences of things are the ideas of God Almighty, they do not have any idependent being of their own. They only subsist in the mind of God. "Relative Not-Being" ('Adam-i-idafī) is the term for not having a real being. It is clear that when there is no being there would be no effects of being too, which are attributes, actions, ownership, etc. The absence of them is spoken of as non-existential attributes. You can intuit this in your being—you think of a friend of yours, his mental image appears before your mind's eye. This, as an idea, is devoid of external existence, and when it does not have even an external existence, it would necessarily be deprived of all the effects of existence. In other words the subsistent is devoid of existence. You possess in yourself being, life, knowledge, power, will, etc., but there are no attributes in the mental picture. The chief reason underlying this is that there is in you Aniyya (I-ness) and Huwiyya (Epseity) and the source of attributes and actions is the same 'Aniyya' and 'Huwiyya'. In the mental image there is neither Aniyya nor Huwiyya. That is the reason why it is deprived of all attributes, actions and effects. Similarly, Aniyya and Huwiyya are peculiar to God Almighty alone, who is the Knower. The essences of things are all 'the known', they are the ideas; they have neither Aniyya nor Huwiyya and due to lack of these they are devoid of all existential attributes and actions.

Now, imagine, when you think of your friend, and his image appears in your mind, all the concomitants of his image, too, then, are conceived, due to which his individuality and identity is determined. The essences of things, or 'ā'yān', cannot be separated from their concomitants, because these are their essential peculiarities; they are related together as logical complements, the separation of the one from the other is inconceivable. The 'known' of God, which are the essences of things, or external realities, together with their concomitants, peculiarites or aptitudes, or, in the terminology of the Qu'rān, 'Shākilāt', subsist in the knowledge of God since Eternity. As they do not have external existence, so they are not termed created, on the contrary they are uncreated. When God's knowledge is eternal, His ideas, objects known, too, will be necessarily eternal, and when these are eternal, their peculiarities or aptitudes too will be eternal and immutable. That is why Shaykh Akbar calls the 'essences, of things (A'yān al thābitā) 'thābitun fi ḥaḍrat al thubūt', that is to say, they remain in their state of latency in the mind of God. Jāmī has expressed it thus :[25]

> Will it be valid to say that the Creator's
> Creativity,
> Creates the aptitudes ?

The question is, when God Almighty is the Knower and the 'essences of things' are His known, latent in His Being alone, and subsisting in His Knowledge only, how are they created in the external ? Note, that things are not created out of nothing, because nothing or not-being does not exist at all, and out of nothing nothing will come. Neither does not-being manifest itself in the form of things, as according to the definition itself pure not-being is not something so that it may constitute the matter out of which a thing may be formed or created, nor is God Almighty divisible in forms, because God's Being is free from divisibility.

Creation is nothing but the external manifestation or actualisation of the ideas of God, or the essences ! The secret of creation, the Ṣūfīs believe, is that God manifests or reveals Himself in His own ideas. In thus manifesting Himself God remains unchanged as ever He was, is, and shall be. God gives and yet preserves Himself, is multiplied and remains one. He manifests Himself according to the 'aptitudes' of the things in which he is manifesting Himself. He bestows His attributes on His ideas or forms or essences and they become things. The essences of things are in themselves non-existent, that is to say, they subsist only in the Knowledge of God as 'ideas'. They derive what existence they possess from God who is the real substance of all that exist. There is really nothing in existence except God. How beautifully Jāmī expresses the whole idea:[26]

The Beloved takes on so many different forms
His beauty expresses itself in varied artistry,
Multiplicity is there to heighten the charm of
  Unity,
The One delights to appear in a thousand garbs.

The same idea has been referred to in the verse :[27]

"God created the heavens and the earth from Ḥaqq. Verily in that is a sign for those who believe."[28] All the ideas or essences of things have appeared from Ḥaqq. According to Sharī'at and the lexical definition, 'Ḥaqq' only is the word for the Absolute Being, and considering derivation, the root of 'Ḥaqq' (God) and 'Ḥaqiqat' (reality), is one and the same. This is the secret of "He is the outward" which is explained by the verse :[29] "God is the Manifest Truth" i.e. God alone is manifest or God alone is 'Ḥaqq' who is manifest. The verse:[31] "God is the Light of the heavens and the earth"[32] further supports it. Reflect and ponder over the above statement !

After briefly presenting these premises I would now turn my attention to an explanation of Evil.

The Ṣūfīs call Ḥaqq, who is pure Existence the absolute Good. Since[33] "God is beautiful and loves beauty" His Being is perfect, His actions are perfect and His attributes are perfect ! That is why He is the Absolute Good. There is not the slightest imperfection here. The essences of things, or the essences of contingent beings, do not exist separately from the Necessary Being. They do not possess either existential attributes or actions of their own and due to this Not-Being they are absolute evil. The assertion of the Ṣūfīs :[34] "Being is absolute good and not-being is absolute evil" has the same meaning. As real being is absolute Good, it necessarily follows that all the existential attributes too are good. If being is good and perfect how can its attributes contain evil or how can they be imperfect ? Hence good will come out of absolute good[35]—"God is Beautiful and nothing but beauty comes out of Him"[36] and conversely if not-being is absolute evil all the non-existential attributes would be evil, therefore, evil will always be evil.[37] "The reality of a thing cannot be separated from it" is an indisputable truth. To regard evil as good is akin to calling black white—it is, as it were, talking rot !

Now after taking note of latent realities or 'essences' of things, pay attention to the external existences of things. Latent realities of things are the determinations of the knowledge of the Absolute Being or in other words, are the ideas of the Absolute Being. Existences of things are the external determinations or modes of this same Absolute Being. In other words, God remaining unchanged in His Being and attributes reveals Himself through the attribute of Light (Nūr) in the forms of the known.

As absolute not-being does not exist, so also Absolute Being does not manifest, because, for manifestation, form or determination is necessary. Now only some aspects of being can appear in forms, and most of them cannot make their appearance. The aspects which manifest themselves are the same whose aptitude the forms possess. Absolute Being manifests itself according to the real aptitudes of forms. Not how Jāmī has clarified this point by the illustration of glasses:[38]

Essences were like glasses variegated in colour,
Red, Yellow and Blue,
The Sun of Being spread its blaze over them,
And came out through them in their colours.

Try to fathom this mystery by the aid of a few illustrations. Note, that unless a point takes the form of a line, surface or circle etc. it is incapable of manifesting itself. Now, in a line, those aspects of a point cannot manifest themselves which appear in the surface. Some of the aspects would necessarily be left out. If a point wants to manifest itself in the alphabetical letters, it would have to adopt the different forms of these letters. Every letter is the form of a point, which leaves out the determinations of the other letters. If the point does not leave off some of its phases, it cannot appear in the form of any letter. If it appears in the form of A, it leaves off all the aspects of B and all the other letters, and similarly, when it manifests itself in the form of B, the aspects of A and all other letters, are left off by it. If the point does not leave off the phase of any letter, it will never be able to make its appearance, because the characteristics of distinction and determination are that it contains something and lacks something. If it contains everything there is no determination and distinction, instead there is indetermination, and if there is nothing, then, it is absolute not-being. In view of the above the letters of the alphabet can address the point thus:[39]

> Thy manifestation is through me and
> my being through thee,
> Without me thou canst not manifest thyself and
> without Thee I could not have come into being.

Now it is, perhaps, clear that creation requires both the Being of God and the subsistence of the essences of created beings (Ideas of God). Both of these are interdependent- 'Ḥaqq' (God) manifests in the form of real objects and objects exist due to the real existence of 'Ḥaqq' (God).[40] "Our being is due to Him and His manifestation is due to us."

Now, again, think over the 'existences' of things. These are manifest because of the immanence of the being of God in them. They are the manifestations, God is manifest in them. The relations, actions and states which appear in the manifestations will be really attributed to God alone, they will be related to 'Ḥaqq' (God). But in view of the manifest and the manifestations, two aspects now come into being viz., the aspect of being and the aspect of not-being. Evil and pain and ugliness which appear in the manifestations are due to their aptitudes and receptivity only. This is the aspect of not-being. The essences of things are 'relative' not-being and not-being is absolute evil; non-existential attributes too are all evil. Manifestation would be in accordance with the aptitudes of essences only i.e. the attributes of Being will appear according to these aptitudes of the essences only, in consequence of this most of the attributes of Being will not be able to manifest themselves. The non-existence of these attributes of Being only is evil; as Being is absolute good, every aspect of Being would be absolute good also. Now the evil which is being fancied in things is due to the non-existence of the attributes of Being (aspect of not-being) otherwise attributes of Being as Being existential aptitudes are good (aspect of being). The whole of this philosophy has been expressed by the eminent Jāmī in the following quatrain:[41]

> Wherever Being's ambit doth extend,
> Good and nought but good is found, O friend,
> All evil comes from not-being, to wit,
> From 'other' and on 'other' must depend!

That is to say, "Being is good and Not-being is evil"[42] and according to the saying "Everything turns towards its origin"[43] it necessarily follows that:[44] "All good is from Being and all evil is from not-being." The same has been referred to in the Tradition:[45] "All good is in Thine Hand and evil is never related to Thee."[46] The following Qur'ānic verse:[47] "Whatever good (oh man) happens to thee is from God; but whatever evil happens to thee is from thy (own) soul."[48] The word "thy soul"[49] implies the aptitudes or receptivity of essence. Jāmī has elucidated it thus:[50]

> All good and all perfection that you see
> Are of the "Truth" which from all stain is free,
> Evil and pain result from some defect,
> Some lack of normal receptivity.

Further, the meaning of "God created you and what ye make"[51] too, becomes quite clear, because action is a necessary concomitant of Being and the same Being is called God. Since creation means 'manifestation' i.e. external revelation and manifestation is a concomitant of Light, (Nūr), which reveals itself and reveals others[52]—and Light (Nūr) is an attribute of God, therefore, Light is nothing but Being itself[53] "God is the Light of the heavens and the earth."[54] To reveal all 'ideas' together with their real aptitudes or peculiarities and acts from the unseen stage into external evidence is a peculiar characteristic of Being which is called Allah (God). Hence the assertion of God in the Qur'ān:[55] "Say, All things are from God."[56]

This reveals the secret of the doctrine:[56] "Every good and evil comes from God."

The followers of J.S. Mill speak of some difficulties in explaining evil. Keeping them in view, let us once more determine the solution offered by the Ṣūfīs. Mill thinks that if we admit God as good and omnipotent, evil could never be explained at all. We have seen that the Ṣūfīs regard God as absolute good, as He is Pure Being, and, therefore, He is All-good. Further when Being is perfect, His attributes, too, will be perfect. Therefore, His will, power, knowledge, etc., will be Perfect in every way. He would be the Absolute Being, Omnipotent and All-knowing too. When God is considered to be All-Good and Omnipotent, how can then He be regarded as the Author of evil? It is inconceivable that Absolute good can cause evil. You have seen above that the Creator of both good and evil is God Almighty[57] "God alone is the Creator of the sheep and the camel and of those who slaughter them." To speak the truth, the Ṣūfīs think, that creation does not mean creation from pure nothing. Creation is a revelation of the essences or quiddities of things in the external world through the attribute of Light (Nūr). Now, as the 'essences' are the ideas of God, so they are eternal and uncreated. If they are not eternal, then, it would necessarily follow, that the knowledge of God, too, is not eternal. When knowledge is not eternal, which is an attribute, Being, too, then, will not be eternal. But the Being of God is eternal, therefore, the ideas or essences also will be eternal. You cannot separate the essences from their aptitudes or real concomitants, consequently they, too, would be eternal and uncreated. Now these essences cannot appear themselves with their real aptitudes and effects. The Being of God (Ḥaqq) alone is the cause of their appearance, that is the reason why the relation of manifestation has been ascribed to the Absolute Being,[58] "All matters go back to God."[59]

You have now discovered the 'Secret of Creation'. Creation is manifestation, revelation—Form or determination or mode is necessary for it. Now, only some attributes of the Absolute Being (God) could be revealed in modes, forms or determinations and many of them are left out; the attributes that are manifesting themselves are doing so in accordance with the aptitudes of the essences. By the attributes which are being left out evil is understood. Evil is another name of not-being.

"All evil comes from not-being, to wit,
From "Other" and on "other" must depend."[60]

The Being of God (Ḥaqq) is the Absolute Being,[61] consequently evil cannot be ascribed to the Being of God: "Evil can never be related to God."

If by creation you understand that a thing could be brought forth from absolute not-being, as J. S. Mill and other philosophers think, then God cannot be regarded as the Creator of evil. But this meaning of the word Creation is preposterous, and nothing could be brought forth from a fantastic absolute not-being. Absolute not-being does not exist at all[62]—"Not-being does not exist." Now you can say with logical consistency that God Almighty is All-good as well as All-powerful. If Being is perfect, all its attributes, too, then will be perfect; admitting Being as perfect attributes could not be regarded as finite or imperfect. The origin of evil is due to our essences which are relative not-being, evil is a concomitant of the relative not-being because determination denotes distinction, here some one or other aspect of Being is left out, which is not-being and that alone is evil[63]—

The bat remonstrated with the Sun.
Asked : "Why do you blind my sight?"
The Sun said: "You have not the power to see.
Blind yourself, yet you remonstrate !"

Now if you reflect on this explanation of the eminent Ṣūfīs you will perhaps find it to be the best solution of the problem of evil.

CHAPTER VII

DIVINE-PRESENCE: INWARD AND OUTWARD EXPERIENCE

> "O ! Allah, Bless me always with the joy of thy Sight and the pleasure of beholding thy countenance, unharmed by anything harmful, undisturbed by anything disturbing."[1-2]

The explanation of the teaching of omnipresence and proximity in its various aspects has been given in the foregoing pages in detail. It is necessary to follow those instructions and strive to master them. Striving or earnest effort alone opens new pathways to God. As the Qur'ān categorically asserts:[3] "As for those who strive in Us, We surely guide them to Our paths."[4] Practice and striving only exalt one in rank:[5] "To each one is a rank according to the deeds which he doeth"[6] and by striving only one can possibly achieve the "Coolness of the eyes", the instructions for whose achievement have been imparted to us by the Prophet of Islam.

The importance of striving could be judged by the response given by Ibrāhīm Adham to a query of Imām Abū Yūsuf. Abū Yūsuf inquired of him, whether it was necessary to learn various sciences for becoming a 'Darwīsh'. Ibrāhīm Adham replied, "Yes, I have heard the tradition that "The love of the world is the root of all evil."[7] I shall learn the other Sciences after following this tradition."

You have read in the foregoing pages that if we regard the Qur'ān and Traditions as a criterion of truth, then, as the text clearly denotes, it is positively and unquestionably proved that:

"God in His Own Immutable State, Attributes and Being, without altering His Individuality, manifests Himself through His attribute of Light, in the form of phenomenal objects, which in reality are but reflected entities expressing outwardly the essences which subsist in the Knowledge of God and hence it is that the Divine Aspects came to be associated with the world of creation or phenomena."

"He is the First and the Last and the Outward and the Inward and He is Knower of all things."[8-9]

After knowing this arcane secret you will have to strive to keep this knowledge always before your mind's eye. In other words you should be able perpetually to feel the intimate Presence of God within and sense the Presence of God without. Your aim should be to feel and sense the Presence of God every moment. Your forgetfulness of God should disappear so that you may be blessed perpetually with His presence and gradually a 'Complete effacement in the Essence of God' may happen.

Keeping this object in view the eminent Jāmī had said:[10]

O heart, thy high-prized learning of the
schools,
Geometry and metaphysic rules—
Yea, all but love of God is devil's lore:
Fear God and leave this lore to fools![11]

And the gnostic of Rūm had said:[12]

Say, is there anyone better than He
Who can give you bliss even for a
moment ?
Neither joy nor power do I seek,
What I desire of Thee is Thee alone !

What means should be adopted to gain this 'Ultima Thule ?' Is this great boon bestowed on one who is 'Elected' by God or could it also be acquired by turning towards Him.

To Practise the Presence of God true knowledge is necessary. You have read above that—

1. The otherness of the 'essences' of created beings is established by the Qur'ān. These 'essences' are externally, 'created' and internally 'known'; they are other than the Essence of God. Therefore to regard the essence of a created being as the Essence of God would be sheer atheism (Ilḥad). The created beings are not God and God is not a created being.

"Glory be to God—I am not one of the idolators."[13-14]

2. The Qur'ān and the Traditions, in spite of this total otherness and clear distinction between the Essence of God and the Essences of the created beings, definitely prove that the Being of God is the First and the Last, the Inward and the Outward, Immanent and Pervading and Omnipresent and near to the essences of the created beings. God is free from the aptitudes of our essences and is still manifesting Himself through the aptitudes of our essences only. To believe in this immanence of God, in spite of His pure transcendence, is perfect faith by which we gain nearness to God. We have now to feel the intimate presence of God within (immanence) and sense the presence of God without (transcendence).

You can explain this knowledge of nearness (in the technical terms of Ṣūfis) thus:

1. Contemplation of the Outward Presence of God, (Naẓar Huwa'l Zahīr) i. e. God alone is manifest in the form of ideas:[15] "You are the Outward and there is nothing above You." Ideas or essences are the mirrors of the Absolute Existence and the Names and Attributes of God, and God alone is manifest in them. In other words the existence of God alone is reflected in the mirrors of the essences and is being multiplied by their effects. According to this insight nothing is visible outwardly save the Being of God, because the existence of God only is manifest by every form of phenomenal things. Shaykh Akbar's words:[16] "Ḥaqq is sensed and Khalq is inferred" express the same truth. In view of this contemplation it has been said:[17] "I never behold anything ere I behold God Himself." The person having such a vision is termed:[18] "The man with the inward eye" by the Ṣūfis.

> Thy Face is Visible through this world,[19]
> who says thou art hidden ?
> If thou art hidden, how then comes in the
> world ?

2. The Meditation of the Inward Immediate Presence of God (Naẓar-i-Huwa'l Bāṭin).

The absolute Existence of God is a mirror and is representing the essences, therefore one sees the essences and Existence is latent i.e. essences are manifest from behind a screen. This stage is that of "believing without seeing."

"Khalq[20] is sensed and Ḥaqq is inferred" expresses the same truth. One having such an insight is called "The man of Reason."[21]

There is a friend of mine behind the screen;
His beauty deserves to be screened !
The world is but the canvas of the painter,
The panoramic phenomena are but the marks
 thereon.[22]
This screen has separated me from thee,
Such is the inherent urge of the screen !

3. The Perfect View, which the Perfect Man is gifted, comprehends both the above mentioned insights; it beholds God in the phenomenal beings and the phenomenal beings in God.

Say I to Him: this screen between
Shall not separate Thee from me ![23]

For such a perfect man the appearance of the multiplicity of phenomenal beings does not prevent him from beholding the unity of God and the beholding of God does not stand in the way of the appearance of the multiplicity of the phenomenal beings. On the other hand, he sees multiplicity in unity and unity in multiplicity. This is spoken of as "Union of Union" (jam'al-jam') and the omnipresence of God with the phenomenal beings is actualised in this state. A person gifted with this insight is called "the man with the inward eye and the man of reason" by the Ṣūfīs:

The clearness of the wine and the
 transparency of the goblet
Have merged one into another !
It is now as it were, all goblet and
 no wine[24]
Or the other way, all wine and no goblet ![25]

Such a perfect man cries out:[26]

Drunk with reality, sober in relation
 to everything beside it,
Every moment a sip of this wine, the
 same moment a touch of sobriety is
 all that I need.

The eminent Jāmī has spoken of all the three insights in the following quatrain:[27]

If thou canst catch the Light of God,
 thou verily art the one with the
 inward eye,
If thou hast failed to catch that
 Light thou mayst at best be the man
 of reason.
Thou wilt certainly be both the man with
 the inward eye and the man of reason,
If thou couldst but see God in His creation,
 the one in the other.

Now, to feel the Presence of God within and sense the Presence of God without perpetually, it is imperative to cultivate this perfect view, this is called "Mūrāqiba-i-Nazarī". This type of meditation has two stages and Makhdūm Sāwī has given them separate names and has briefly determined the meaning of each of them.[28]

1. Contemplation of things Phenomenal (Mūrāqiba-i-Khalq)

To practise this contemplation you should observe the 'form' of everything and be firmly convinced that all these things are the shadows or reflections of the ideas of God or essences of things which are reflected in the mirror of the Existence of God. Further you should believe that they have revealed themselves after being ascribed with divine attributes viz. Life, Knowledge, Will, Power, Hearing, Sight, Speech etc. In brief, you should firmly believe that everything exists by the Existence of God. Makhdūm says by the constant practice of this contemplation one can promptly discover the essences of things, which are the reality of all the phenomenal beings, and can behold the Divine Throne ('Arsh), the Foot Stool (Kūrsi), the Preserved Tablet (Lauḥ-i-Maḥfūz), the Pen (qalum), Angels etc. This is what is called "Clairvoyant illumination" [Kashf-e-Kaunī].

2. Contemplating the Divine (Mūrāqiba-i-Ḥaqq)

To practise this type of Contemplation, one should be firmly convinced that the existence of the things in space and time perceptible by the outward or inward senses is nothing but the Existence of God that, in accordance with the beautiful and glorious Names of God, has revealed Itself in the mirror of the essences of things i.e. in their form and shape. In other words, God subsisting in His own self and possessing His attributes, without any change, has manifested Himself in the form of phenomenal things through the attribute of Light. Speaking tersely, all this is God and God alone who is manifest in these shapes and forms. "You are the Outward and there is nothing above you."[29]

Do not get puzzled over the variegated
aspects of thy Friend ![30]
Look ! In every aspect He alone is manifest !

Then, after thus observing the Huwiyya and Anniya of God, one should turn towards his own self and deny his own Anniya and Huwiyya. Closing his eyes he should contemplate that he whom he knew was not his ownself but that is none other than God who has manifested Himself in that form: "I do not exist, God alone exists."[31] If God wills, this finding of God in the secret place (within) and contemplating the Divine (without) will produce a state of "Self-forgetfulness". Now, the observer and the observed become one, the Veil is lifted off and one gains the proximity of God. This is called "The intensity of the Consciousness of the Inward" (Ghalabā-i-Huwal Bātīn). This is what is meant by "Perfect poverty is God indeed !"[32]

He alone is the Observer, He alone the
Observed ![33]
There is none but He in the world of
Existence.

This is "Effacement" (Maḥwiat) a "retrocession of the trust." Now the 'abd does not become God. The 'abd does not exist at all, God is all in all.

God stayed back, the rest passed away !
By God ! nothing exists save God ![34]

In short, an accomplished gnostic, who is a perfect preceptor also, explains to you this subtle point that "God in His Own Immutable State without altering this Individuality manifests Himself through His attribute of Light in the form of phenomenal objects". And by the grace of God you firmly believe in it, and according to his instructions you always try to keep it in view. At the outset you do not succeed in this attempt, most of your time is spent in forgetfulness and at times you remember God. This is the preliminary stage.

But you have to persevere and persevere again! You have to give your whole life to prayer, contemplation and communion with God, feeling His intimate presence within and sensing His Presence without. The following couplets of the gnostic of Rūm, which express an unchangeable law will encourage you:[35]

Keep up strenuously toiling along
This path,
Do not rest till the last breath.
Toil on till the last breath; for
That last breath may yet bring the
blessing from the Knower of all
things!
Thy Friend keeps dear thy restless
strivings,
Even hectic activity is better than
sluggish slumber!
Do something, do not grow indolent.
Dig out the earth from the well bit
by bit.
If you could but keep on from day to
day,
You surely will one day reach the water
clear as crystal.
If you fix your seat at some one's street
corner,
You are sure to come one day face to face
with him!

On account of your sincerity and constant turning towards God, your 'forgetfulness' gradually leaves you and 'remembrance' takes its place instead. The thought of God becomes confirmed and just as the Knowledge of God had taken hold of your mind so also the remembrance of God takes firm roots in your heart. When this contemplation reaches its climax, you are then not forgetful of God for even a moment. Perpetually you are in the Presence of God. This stage is spoken of as "Yāddāsht" by the Ṣūfīs. If God wills, the practice of this kind of contemplation will reveal to you that 'State' which is expressed by the Prophet in these words:[36]

"I have sometimes a moment in God which neither the most intimate angels of God nor his Messengers can attain thereto."

O God ! raise us to this stage of life !

Remember well the unveiling of the meaning of "He is the Outward"[37] is possible by the word of a perfect preceptor. The apparent eye can see that God alone is revealing and manifesting Himself in the form of phenomenal things; but the revelation of God's inwardness [huwal Bātīn] is dependent on the contemplation of "He is the Outward."[38] If one is acquired by "talk", the other is gained by "work;" if one is explained by 'knowledge' the other is acquired by 'experience'. If one is found by 'hearing', the other is discovered by 'sight'; if one is unveiled by the 'eye of the head', the other is seen by the 'eye of the mind'. If one is revealed by words, the other is realised by 'experience [ḥāl]. Therefore the fortunate person who has acquired the knowledge of "He is the Outward"[39] should not be content with it but busy himself in acquiring the experience of God's inwardness [huwal Bātīn], because without work and earnest effort the acquirement of the experience of God's inwardness is impossible and this work consists merely in sensing the intimate Presence of God within and sensing the Presence of God without.

In this connection Jāmī emphasises: "It is necessary for thee to habituate thyself to this intimate relation such-a-wise that at no time and in no circumstances thou mayest be without the sense of it, either in coming or going, in eating or sleeping, in speaking or listening. In short, thou must ever be on the alert both when resting and when working, not to waste thy time in insensibility [to this relation]—nay, more, thou must watch every breath, and take heed that it goeth not forth in negligence:

The years roll on: Thou showst not
Thy face,[40]
Yet nothing from my breast Thy love
can chase,
Thine image ever dwells before my eyes,
And in my heart Thy love, aye, holds its
place."[41]

If God wills, this will make the spiritual insight keener. Now, in every form you will behold a spectacle of real beauty and glory and will find joy in every glance you cast. Having this importance of practice in view Jāmī has said:[41]

If thou shouldst care to enter the
ranks of the men of vision,
Thou shouldst pass from the stage of
talking on to the stage of feeling !
Thou dost not become a unitarian by the
mere talk of the unity of God !
The mouth doth not get sweet by the
mere talk of sugar !

Somewhere else he says explicitly:[42]

O Thou, who art the quintessence of the
world !
Thou canst not realise the unity of God
by the mere word of mouth !
What thou canst not gain by the mere
reading of Fuṣūṣ and Lam'āt,
Thou canst indeed achieve by a direct
denial of thine own existence !

We do not in the least underestimate "the stage of talking". By true knowledge only can gnosis be acquired. The true knowledge alone teaches us that we are supplicants [faqīr]. Possession and power, actions, attributes and existence do not really belong to us. Being supplicants we gain the distinction of 'trust'. By knowing the aspects of 'want' and 'trust' the words:[43] "Glory be to God—I am not one of the idolators" are actualized i.e., we do not believe the things attributed to God could be attributed to us too, and thus we steer clear of false worship [Shirk] and do not ascribe our things [non-existential attributes, imperfections] to God, which would affect His transcendence and we may be branded as unbelievers [Kāfirs]. We posit God Almighty's things for Him alone, and sincerely believe in real unification. As a consequence of 'want' and 'trust' we acquire 'vicegerency' and 'saint-ship'. When we employ the divine trusts versus the universe we are called the vicegerent of God and when we make use of them in relation to God we are termed the 'saint' [wali] of God. By "talk" only are we able to gain the knowledge of the real worth of 'abd. Is not, then, this knowledge important? Further, by means of this knowledge we can feel God within and sense God without—in the universe, whenever we like.

Now, what is the nature of Striving or earnest effort or work? It is nothing but a representation to mind of the same knowledge. It does not consist in devotional prayers for 'forty days', giving up of the rights of self and renouncing one's own wife and children! Remember that for this "representation" thanksgiving, prayer, dependence on God, submission, patience and resignation are essential. If these are made the basis of striving, it is no wonder that God would favour one with the dual experience of feeling and sensing God within and without and make him his 'selected one'. The method you will have to follow will be that every day:

[1] You should offer thanks: you should say "O, God Almighty! By your Grace and Mercy You have rid me of the ignorance of the true nature of myself and have enlightened my mind with the light of perfect faith. You alone have showed me that you yourself are the Outward, the Inward, the First and Last of everything! The aim of my life is the realisation of your Divine Presence!

[2] Pray to God: "O, God Almighty! By Your grace and mercy bestow on me the blessing of Your perpetual remembrance! Remove my forgetfulness and oblivion. You have said:[44] "Pray unto me and I will hear your prayer."[45] With all humility I beseech you to be within my reach and reveal to me the secret of Your "Inwardness".

[3] Dependence on God and Submission: "O, God Almighty! To achieve my object I have wholly entrusted myself

to Your care. I have entrusted this major task to You only, You alone are able to cope with it.

"And alone is God as a disposer of affairs."[46-47]

[4] Patience: "O, God Almighty ! I suffer patiently the pain, agony and anxiety caused to me by the slowness in achieving my object. I know that you are aware of my condition and Benevolent to me. You are Omnipotent, too, and this tardiness has some wisdom in it, which on the whole is beneficial to me. In view of my patience and perseverance I implore You to bless me with Your Divine Companionship as You have promised:[48] "God is *with* those who patiently persevere."[49]

[5] Resignation: O, God, Almighty ! The forgetfulness experienced by me is related to my 'essence' which subsist in Your knowledge. You are expressing Yourself just in accordance with it. I submit humbly to this Divine Decree—

"I surrender to the Lord and Cherisher of the Universe."[51]

O, Almighty God ! I strive to feel Your Presence within and sense Your Presence without and I am convinced that I shall ultimately succeed in achieving my object. This has been promised by You, too;

"As for those who strive in Us we surely guide them to Our paths."[52-53]

We found that the fruit of gnosis is "Vision". After knowing the secret—'He is the Outward'[54]—you see Reality expressing itself in every form:[55] "And whithersoever ye turn there is Allah's Countenance."[56] Allah's countenance alone is the Real Existence which reveals itself in the form of phenomenal things and every moment you are beholding Allah's Countenance !

Now, the sum and substance of this gnosis is love. So long as there is ignorance there is no vision; love, too, is not possible. When ignorance is got rid of, the knowledge of Divine Presence is gained. A natural outcome of it is love and truly speaking the faithful cannot love anyone save God. "Those who believe are stauncher in their love for Allah (only)."[57-58]

The fruit of this love is joy, so the more a gnostic loves God, the more joy will he derive from the vision of His Countenance. The more the gnosis is pure and plentiful, the more will the vision be complete and vivid, and the stronger the love, the more complete would the joy be. Hence, the joy of vision enjoyed by the prophets is denied to saint and that enjoyed by saints is not allowed to 'Ulamā [Theologians]. In short, there would be difference in vision and joy according to the purity and strength of gnosis and love. If in vision the gnostics be even alike, then, too, there could be difference in their joy. A simple illustration can make it clear and easily comprehensible. Two men are gazing at a lovely damsel. The sight of both of them is equally keen. One of them is the lover and the other only an observer. It is obvious that the observer cannot enjoy even one tenth of the pleasure afforded to the lover by her sight. That is the reason why love and devotion are necessary with the gnosis of God. Jāmī has expressed this idea thus:[59]

Once you attain gnosis, learn to strive
along the path of love !
To be a gnostic is to be but a kernel but
to be a lover is to be the very core
of the kernel !

The Holy Prophet, by the following prayer:[60]

"O Allah ! Bless me always with the joy of thy Sight and the pleasure of beholding thy Countenance" is teaching us to demand the Same love from God, as there would not be vision without gnosis, and joy is impossible without vision and love. It is evident that when a man does not possess knowledge of a thing, he would not be curious to have a vision of it, and when one is not keen on doing so, one would not derive any pleasure from vision. Therefore the essence of pleasure is love and love is dependent on vision and vision without knowledge is impossible. It is clear that gnosis and love and knowledge and devotion are necessary and the important outcome of these is joy and pleasure.

When together with perfect gnosis, the feelings of love and devotion are created in the mind of a gnostic then he, residing in this world only, enters into Heaven. This gnostic is thus addressed "Enter thou among my bondsmen ! Enter thou My Garden."[61-62] As soon as his state of 'abidyat is actualized, he steps into the Heaven of Dhāt ! Being closely placed to the fountain of the Nearness to God, he is always intoxicated with the wine of love. "A spring whence those brought near to Allah drink"[63-64] and his prayer is granted in which he had requested:[65]

"O God ! I seek of thee a bounty that never perisheth and a coolness of the eye that never ceases !"

"This indeed is the bliss of life in this world and in the Hereafter !" "O God ! raise us to this state of life."

REFERENCES

CHAPTER I

1. The Doctrines of the Sufis or *Kitab al-Ta'arruffl madhahab ahl al-tasawwuf,* translated from the Arabic of Abu Bakr al-Kala'badhi by Arthur John Arberry, Cambridge University Press, 1930 p. 5 : referred to in future as D.S.

2. ألا إن فی جسد بنی آدم مضغة اذا اصلحت صلح الجسد کله
واذا فسدت فسد الجسد کله ، ألا هی القلب (رواه البخاری)

3. Ibid-p. 9.

4. الصفا من الله انعام واکرام و الصوف لباس الانعام

5. اتباع تابعین 6. صحابیت 7. صحابه

8. الصوفی من لبس الصوف علی الصفا وافاق الهوی طعم الجفا ولزم
طریق المصطفی وکانت الدنیا منه علی القفا۔

9. Ibid-p. 10.

10. التصوف هو علم تعرف به احوال تزکیة النفوس وتصفیة الاخلاق
وتعمیر الظاهر والباطن لنیل السعادة الابدیة ، موضوعه
التزکیة و التصفیة والتعمیر، وغایته نیل السعادة الابدیه

11. الصفا محمود بکل لسان وضده الکدورة هی مذمومة

12. عن ابی حجیفة ، قال : خرج علینا رسول الله صلی الله علیه وسلم
متغیر اللون ، فقال : ذهب صفو الدنیا وبقی الکدر، فالموت الیوم
تحفة لکل مسلم .

13. اے دل طلب کمال در مدرسہ چند
تکمیل اصول وحکمت وہندسہ چند
ہر فکر کہ جز ذکر خدا وسوسہ است
شرمے ز خدا بدار این وسوسہ چند

14. *Lawa'ih,* Flash II, Trans. by E.H. Whinfield.

15. التصوف ترك كل حظ للنفس

16. The *Kashf al-Mahjub* By 'Ali B. 'Uthman Al-Julla'-bi Al-Hujwiri, translated into English by Dr. R.N. Nicholson, (London, 1936) P. 37.

17. ولا تتبع الهوى فيضلك عن سبيل الله

18. نیکو مثلے شنوز پیر بسطام

ازدانه طمع ببرکه رستی ازدام

19. التصوف هو الأخلاق الرضية 20. Ibid—p. 43.

21. الاعراض عن الاعمراض 22. *Rasa'il Qushariya,* p. 128.

23. هو الدخول فى كل خلق سنى والخروج من كل خلق دنى

24. التصوف اخلاق كريم ظهرت فى زمان كريم من رجل

25. Ibid—p. 127. كريم مع قوم كريم

26. التصوف خلق فمن زاد عليك فى الخلق فقد زاد عليك فى الصفا

27. *Kashf al-Mahjub* p. 39. 28. D.S. pp. 43-44.

29. S. II. 129. والذين جاهدوا فينا لنهدينهم سبلنا

30. S. XXIX, 69.

يا ايها الذين آمنوا اتقوا الله وابتغوا اليه الوسيلة وجاهدوا فى سبيله لعلكم تفلحون .

31. S.V. 38. 32. D.S. p. 46.

33 & 34. *Rasa'il Qushayriya* p. 26. 35.

36. For an explanation see Chap. 3.

37 فلا تنظر العين إلا اليه ولا يقع الحكم الا عليه

38. Ibid. 39. *Rasa'il Qushayriya* p. 127.

40 ان يكون العبد فى كل وقت بما هوا اولى به فى الوقت

41. اے آن کہ بقبلۂ بتان روست ترا

برمغز چرا حجاب شد پوست ترا

دل درپے این و آن نہ نیکوست ترا

یک دل داری بس است یک دوست ترا (جامی)

42. *Lawa'ih* Flash I, Translated by E.H. Whinfield.

43. استرسال النفس مع الله تعالى على مايريد

44. *Rasa'il Qushayriya* p. 127.

45. ساكن الجوارح مطمئن الجنان مشروح الصدر منورا الوجه

عامر البطن غنيا من الاشياء لخالقها .

46. *Futuh-al-Ghayb*, Chap. 6.

47. التصوف الاخذ بالحقائق واليأس مما فى ايدى الخلائق

48. R.Q.P. 127.

49. الصوفى منقطع عن الخلق ومتصل بالحق لقوله تعالى 'واصطنعتك

لنفسى ، قطعه من كل غير ، ثم قال : ' لن ترانى '

50. Ibid.—p. 127. 51. S. XX, 41.

52. S. VII, 143. 53 هم قوم آثروا الله عزوجل على كل شئ

54. Ibid.

55. ز آمیزش جان و تن توی مقصودم

وز مردن و زیستن توی مقصودم

تو دیر بزی کہ من برقسم زمیان

گر من گویم ز من توی مقصودم

56. *Lawa'ih* Flash, VI.

57. إياك نعبد وإياك نستعين 58. S.I., 4.

59. S. LVI. 89. 60. فليعلم انا نعنى بالصوفية المقربين

61. افغير الله تتقون 62. S. XVI, 52. 63. هل من خالق غير الله

64. S. XXXV, 3. 65.

65. For Quranic Verses and the Traditions of the Prophet in support of it, see the 3rd Chap. of this book.

66. یاایها الناس انتم الفقراء الی الله والله هو الغنی الحمید

67. S. XXXV. 15.

68. هوالحی القیوم   69. S. II, 254.

70. هوالعلیم القدیر   71. S. XXX, 54.

72. هوالسمیع البصیر   73. S. XVII, 1

74. مایزال عبد یتقرب الی بالنوافل حتی احبته، واذا احبته کنت
سمع الذی یسمع به وبصره الذی یبصربه ویده التی یبطش به
ورجله التی یمشی بها (رواه البخاری)

75. *Bukhari.*

76. فؤاده الذی یعقل به ولسانه الذی یتکلم به (شرح مشکوٰة

77. *Mishkat.*   78. ع نامے است بمن زمن وباقی همه اوست

79. علمنا هذا مشید بالکتاب والسنة   80. الیأس مما فی ایدی الناس

81. B. Macdonald: *Development of Muslim Theology* p. 180.

82. S. IV. 150.

83. چراغ مرده کجا شمع آفتاب کجا
ببین تفاوت راه از کجا است تا بکجا (حافظ)

84. من یدر ما قلت لم تخزل بصیرته
ولیس یدریه إلا من له بصر

CHAPTER II

1. اے دردل من اصل تمنا همه تو
اے درسر من مایه سودا همه تو
هر چند به روزگار در می نگرم
امروز همه توی و فردا همه تو (ابوسعید مهنه)

2. من باغ جہان را قفسے دیدم وبس
مرغش زہوا وہو سے دیدم وبس
از صبح وجود تا شبان گاہ عدم
چون چشم کشودم نفسے دیدم وبس (سحابی استرآبادی)

3. ہستی کہ عیان نیست دو آن درشانے
درشان دگر جلوہ کند ہر آنے
این نکتہ بجوز "کل یوم ہو فی شان"
گر بایدت از کلام حق برہانے

4. ذل وافتقار 5. عبادت 6. استعانت

7. لا الہ اللہ محمد رسول اللہ

9. فلا تخافوھم وخافون ان کنتم مؤمنین 10. S. III, 175.

11. الیس اللہ بکاف عبدہ 12. S. XXXIX, 35.

13. لکیلا تأسوا علی ما فاتکم ولا تفرحوا بما آتاکم 14. S. LVII, 23.

15. انتم الأعلون واللہ معکم 16. S. III, 138.

17. ضعف الطالب والمطلوب 18. S. XXI, 7.

19. افغیر اللہ تامرونی اعبد أیہا الجاھلون 20. S. XXXIX, 64.

21. کان بالمؤمنین رحیما 22. S. XXXIII, 42

23. کفی باللہ وکیلا 24. فاتخذہ وکیلا

25. ومایستوی الأعمی والبصیر والظلمات ولا النور ولا الظل
ولا الحرور ومایستوی الاحیاء ولا الاموات

26. S. XXXV 19-22 27. انی ذاھب الی ربی سیھدین

28. S. XXXII, 78 29. اللہ اکبر

31. انی وجھت وجھی للذی فطر السموات والارض حنیفا

32. S. VI. 79. وما انا من المشركين
33. The opening prayer recited in "Salat"
34. لا اله غيرك 36. الحمد لله رب اللعالمين 37. S.I, I.
38. رب العالمين 39. S.I, I. 40. لا رب سواه
42. الرحمن الرحيم 43. S.I, 2.44. 44. كان ما لمؤمنين رحيما
45. S. XXXIII, 42. 46. مالك يوم الدين 47. S.I, 3.
48. يوم لا تملك نفس لنفس شيئا 49. S. LXXXII-19.
50. إياك نعبد 51. S.I, 4. 52. إياك نستعين 53. S.I, 4.
54. اهدنا الصراط المستقيم 55. S. 15.
56. صراط الذين انعمت عليهم غير المغضوب عليهم ولا الضالين
57. S.I, 6.
58. سمع الله لمن حمده 59. جعلت قرة عيني في الصلواة
60. نعم المولى ونعم النصير 61. S. VIII, 39.
62. واعتصموا بالله هو مولكم نعم المولى ونعم النصير
63. S. XXII, 78.
64. لا قوة الا بالله 65. S. XVIII, 38.
66. لاحول ولا قوة الا بالله 67. Hadith. 68.
68 لا تتحرك ذرة الا باذن الله 69. Hadith.
70. اسلمت لرب العالمن 71. S. II, 120.
72. ادعوني استجب لكم 73. لا تايئسوا من روح الله
74. S. XII-8.

75. گر مراد تو اے دوست نامرادی ما است
مراد خویش دگر بار می بخواہم خواست

76. عسى ان تكرهوا شيئا و هو خير لكم وعسى ان تحبوا شيئا

وهو شر لكم والله يعلم وانتم لا تعلمون .

77. S. II, 216. 78. لكل اجل كتاب 79. S. XIII. 38.

80. ان العبد يرى فى صحائفه يوم القيامة حسنات لا يعرفها فيقال انها بدل سؤالك فى الدنيا لم يقدر قضاؤه فيها (الحديث)

81. اللهم اكفنى كل مهم من حيث شئت وكيف شئت وأنى شئت ومن أين شئت

وكلت الى المحبوب أمرى كله

فان شاء أحيانى وان شاء أتلفا

83. لاحول ولا قوة الا بالله 85. اعتصام بالله

86. لا قوة الا بالله 87. S. XVII, 39.

88. وما من دآبة فى الارض إلّا على الله رزقها 89. S. XI, 6.

90. وفى السماء رزقكم وما توعدون فورب السمآء والارض انه لحق مثل ما انكم تنطقون .

91. S. LI, 22-23.

92. ومن يتق الله يجعل له مخرجا ويرزقه من حيث لا يحتسب ومن يتوكل على الله فهو حسبه .

93.

94. بدنبال روزی چه باید دوید

تو بنشین که روزی خود آید پدید

95. پس توکل کن مارزان پا و دست

رزق تو بر تو ز تو عاشق تراست

96. بعد از طلب می یابی امانه بطلب می یابی

97. بجستجوے نیابد کسے مراد دلی

کسے مراد بیابد که جستجو دارد

98. اف لدنيا ولأيامها فانها للحزن مخلوقة

همومها لاتقضى ساعة   عن ملك فيهااوالسومه

99. لقد خلقنا الانسان فى كبد 100. S. 90, 3.

101. انه هو أضحك وأبكى S. 53,42,43,47.

102. انه هو أمات وأحيا 103. انه هو أغنى وأقنى 104. صبر

105. يا ايها الذين آمنوا اصبروا وصابروا ورابطوا واتقوا الله لعلكم تفلحون .

106. S. III. 200.

107. گرگریزی باامید راحتے
هم از انجا پیشت آید آفتے
هیچ کنجے بے ددو بے دام نیست
جز بخلوت گاه حق آرام نیست

108. ولربك فاصبر 109. S. LXXIV. 7.

110. عسى ان تكرهوا شيئا و يجعل الله فيه خيرا كثيرا

111. S. IV. 19. 112. الحمد لله على مايساء ويسر

113. فلما رأينه اكبرنه وقطعن ايديهن 114. S. XII, 31.

115. حفت الجنة بالمكاره وحفت النار بالشهوات

116. ومن يعش عن ذكر الرحمن نقيض له شيطانا فهوله قرين

117. S. XLIII, 35. 118. إنى فعال لما اريد

119. واصبر لحكم ربك فانك بأعيننا 120. S. 52, 48.

121. اذا احب الله عبد ابتلاه فان صبر اجتبا وان رضى اصطفاه

122. والله يحب الصابرين 123. XIII, 146.

124. ان الله مع الصابرين 125. S. II. 153.

126. وجعلنا منهم ائمة يهدون بامرنا لما صبروا وكانوا باياتنا يوقنون

128. وان تصبروا وتتقوا لايضركم كيدهم شيئا 129. - S. III 120.

130. فاصبران العاقبة للمتقين 131. S. XI, 40.

132. انما يوفى الصابرون أجرهم بغير حساب

134. وبشر الصابرين الذين اذا اصابتهم مصيبة قالوا إنا لله وانا اليه راجعون اولئك عليهم صلوة من ربهم ورحمة واولئك هم المهتدون

135. S. II, 155-156.

136. زہر غم دوست جز شکر نیست

این تیر نصیب ہر جگر نیست

بد کے دہد آن حبیب جانی

شیرین بود انچہ تلخ دانی

137. يتعاهد الله عبده بالبلاء كما يتعاهد الوالد اشفق ولده

138. انما اشكو بثي وحزني الى الله 139. S. XII, 86.

140. دردم نہان بہ زطبیبان مدعی

باشد کہ از خزانہ غیبم دوا کنند

141. ہر چہ آن خسرو کند شیرین بود ؎

142. جہان دارد اند جہان داشتن ؎

143. لئن شكرتم لازيدنكم 144. S. XIV, 7.

145. من نزلت اليه نعمة فليشكرها

146. النعمة وحتية فقيدوها بالشكر

147. حافظ 148. جالب

149. يا ايها الظالم فى فعله

والظلم مردود على من ظلم

الى متى حتى متى

تشكو المصيبات وتنسى النعم

150. نعمت نفع 151. نعمت دفع

152. نعمت توفیق 153. نعمت عصمة

154. بے لطف تو من قرار نتوانم کرد
احسان تو شمار نتوانم کرد
گر بر تن من زبان شود ہر موے
یک شکر تو از ہزار نتوانم کرد

155. Translated by R.A. Nicholson in Studies in Mysticism, p. 51.

156. ان تعدّوا نعمة الله لا تحصوها S. XIV, 33.

158. فانه كان للاوّابين غفورا 159. S. XVII, 24.

160. إني لغفّار لمن تاب وآمن وعمل صالحا ثم اهتدى 161. S. XX, 82.

162. ان الله يحب التوابين S. II, 222.

163. لا قوّة الا بالله S. XVIII, 39.

164. فاذكروني اذكركم 165. S. II, 152.

166. رضي الله عنهم ورضوا عنه S. V. 123.

آنان کہ رضائے حق بجان می جویند
در راہ رضائے او بسر می پویند
ہر یک ہمہ آن کند کہ حق فرماید
حق نیز ہمان کند کہ ایشان گویند

168. لا اله الا الله، محمد الرسول الله

170. ایمان 171. بدعة

172 كل بدعة ضلالة 173. کفر

174. گر تو خواہی حری و دل زندگی
بندگی کن بندگی کن بندگی

زندگی مقصود بہر بندگی است
زندگی بے بندگی شرمندگی است
جز خضوع و بندگی و اضطرار
اندرین حضرت ندارد اعتبار
ہر کہ اندر عشق یابد زندگی
کفر باشد پیش او جز بندگی
ذوق باید تا دہد طاعات بر
مغز باید تا دہد دانہ شجر

175. قل هذه سبيلي ادعوا الى الله على بصيرة انا من اتبعني وسبحان الله وما انا من المشركين

176. XII. 108.

CHAPTER III

1. در کون و مکان نیست عیان جز یک نور
ظاہر شدہ آن نور بانواع ظہور
حق نور تنوع ظہورش عالم
توحید ہمیں است دگر وہم و غرور

2. هوالاول والآخر والظاهر والباطن وهو بكل شئ عليم

3. S. LVII, 3.

4. فلفی گشتی و آگہ فیستی
خود کجا و از کجا و نیستی
از خود آگہ چون نہ اے بے شعور
پس نیاید بر چنیں علمت غرور

5. بود نور خرد در ذات انوار
بسان چشم سر در چشمہ خور

6. عقل رہبر ولیک تا در او

وآن عنایت رساندت بر وا

7. چون بدانی تو کماہی خویش را

علم عالم حاصل آید مر ترا

گر ہمی خواہی کہ باشی حق شناس

خویش رابشناس نہ زراہ قیاس

بل زاراہ کشف وتحقیق ویقین

عارف خود شو کہ حتی دانی است این

8. انما امرہ اذا اراد شیئا ان یقول لہ کن فیکون 9. S. XXXVI, 82.

10. وقد خلقتك من قبل ولم تك شیئا 11. S. XIX, 9.

12. الا یعلم من خلق وھو اللطیف الخبیر 13. S. LXVII, 14.

14. وھو الخلاق العلیم 15. S. XXXVI, 80.

16. وھو بکل خلق علیم 17. S. XXXVI, 78.

18. اللہ خالق کل شئی

20. لم تك شیئا 21. S. XIX, 9.

22. عدم اضافی 23. شاکلات

24. سبحانہ تعالی عما یصفون 25. لیس کمثلہ شئی وھو السمیع البصیر

26. یحذرکم اللہ نفسہ (S. III, 28)

27 انہ لیس للعبد فی العبودیۃ نہایۃ حتی یصل الیھا ثم یرجع ربا کما انہ لیس للرب حد ینتھی الیہ ثم یعود عبدا فالرب رب غیر نہایۃ والعبد عبد غیر نہایۃ

28. Chap. XXVII.

29. والرب رب ان تنزّل 30. العبد عبد وان ترقی

31. Gulshan-i-Raz, Trans. by Whinfield, 508-11

32. صوفیہ کا یاد رکھ قاعدہ کلیہ
خلق نہ ہوجائے حق، عبد نہ ہوجاے رب
عطر کو کہنا شراب اور آب کو کہنا سراب
خوب کو کہنا خراب، کذب ہے اے بے ادب
کر تو حقیقی دوی عالم و حق میں ثبوت
ورنہ حقائق کے بیچ لاف نہ کر مرتد لب

33. الحق موجود، العبد معدوم، وقلب الحقائق محال، فالحق حق والعبد عبد

34. عبد سو عبد ہے اللہ سو اللہ مدام
حاشا اللہ نہ کبھی عابد و معبود ہمہ اوست

35. یا ایها الناس انتم الفقراء الی الله و الله هو الغنی الحمید ۔

36. S. XXXV, 15. 37. لا اله الا الله محمد رسول الله

38. لا اله الا الله

39. هر انکس را که ایزد راه نه نمود
ز استعمال منطق هیچ نه کشود

40. Gulshan-i-Raz, Trans. by E.H. Whinfield, 1189, 90.

41. وهو معكم اينما كنتم والله بما تعملون بصير

42. S. LVII, 4. 43. بما تعملون بصير

44. يستخفون من الناس ولا يستخفون من الله وهو معهم

45. S. IV, 108. 46. الله 47. الله معنا

48. هو 49. هو معكم

50 اذا كان احدكم يصلى فلا يبصق قبل وجهه اذ اصلى، فان الله تبارك تعالى قبل وجهه اذا صلى ۔

51. فیه الرد علی من زعم انه علی العرش بذاته

52. او با شما است ہر جا که باشید 53. الله معی

54. Qaul-al-Jamil (Cairo Edition, 1290 A.H.) p. 20.

55. آیات کلام الله و احادیث رسول الله صلعم معیت و قرب ذاتی صریحا اثبات می کنند .... ہمه انصاف است که منصوصات شرع را غیر شرعی و مخیلات عقل ناقص خود را شرعی نام کنیم !

56. نحن اقرب الیه منکم ولاکن لاتبصرون 57. S. LVI, 85.

58. لاتعلمون 59. لاتعقلون 60. لاتبصرون

61. S.L., 16.

62. ونعلم ماتوسوس به نفسه ونحن اقرب الیه من حبل الورید

63. واذا سالك عبادی عنی فانی قریب 64. S. II. 186.

65. ان اعرابیا قال : یارسول الله اقریب ربنا فنناجیه ام بعید فنناديه ؟ فسکت النبی صلی الله علیه وسلم فانزل الله اذا سالك عبادی عنی فانی قریب

66. خواب جہل از حرم قرب مرا دور فگند
ورنه نزدیک تر از دوست کسے ہیچ ندید!

67. عن ابی موسی الاشعری فقال : کنا مع رسول الله صلعم فی سفر، فجعل الناس یجهرون بالتکبیر، فقال رسول الله صلعم : یا ایها الناس ! اربعوا علی انفسکم انکم لاتدعون اصما ولا غائبا انکم تدعون سمیعا بصیرا وهو معکم، والذی تدعونه اقرب الی احدکم من عنق راحلته (متفق علیه)

68. Muslim & Bukhari. 69. ماکنا غائبین 70. S. VII, 7.

71. فانی قریب 72. S. II, 186.

73. Muktubat-Vol. I. Muktub 25.

74. نحن اقرب ازکتاب حق بخوان
نسبت خود را بحق نیکو بدان
هست حق از ما بما نزدیک تر
ما ز دوری گشته جویان دربدر

75. نحن اقرب منکم

76. لا بالمکان ولا بالزمان ولا بالرتبة بل بالذات من غیر اختلاط ولا حلول ولا اتحاد ۔

77. Tabsir-al-Qur'an (Cairo Edition p. 319).

78. چون دانستی که حقیقت این است معلوم تو شد که قرب و بعد مسافت همه از توهم است کئے دوری بود تا نزدیکی حاصل شود ، کئے جدائی داشت تا پیوستگی پیدا کند
(رسالہ نور وحدت)

79. Risala Nur Wahdat.

80. الا انه بکل شئ محیط

81. S. IV, 126.

82. وکان الله بکل شئ محیطا

83. S. XLI, 54.

84. سبحانه وتعالی عن تکیف من زعم ان الهنا محدود فقد جهل الخالق المعبود ومن ذکر ان الاماکن به تحیط الزمه الحیرة والتخلیط ، بل هو محیط بکل مکان ۔

85. Abu Na'ym.

86. قال : کان سفیان الثوری وشعبه وحماد سلمه وشریك وابوعوانة لایحدون ولایشبهون ولایمثلون ۔

87. من حصر الله تعالی فی الجهة الفوقیة اوالتحیته فقد کفر

88. حرام علی العقول ان یحدونه و یمثلونه ۔

89. وان الله قد احاط بكل شئ علما 90. S. LXV, 12.

91. كان الله بكل شئ محيطا 92. S. IV, 126.

93. فاينما تولوا فثم وجه الله 94. S. II, 115.

هولا كيف ولا اين له

95. وهو فى كل النواحى لايزول

96. هر جا كه ايستاده روے خود را بسوے او گردانيد ومتوجه شويد پس در همون مكان است حضور خدا وقرب او

97. كل شئ هالك الا وجه 98. S. XXVIII,

99. كل من عليها فان

100. S. LV, 26, 27. 101. فاينما تولوا فثم وجه الله

102. Sirat-al-Musta-qim. Chap. 4.

103. حضرت وجود نفس ذات است تعالى وتقدس

104. وجوده عين ذاته

105. ان الله على كل شئ شهيد 106. S. XXII, 17.

107. الشهيد الحاضر الذى لا يغيب عنه معلوم ولا مرئى ولا مسموع

108. وما تكون فى شان وتتلوا منه من قرآن ولا تعملون من عمل الا كنا عليكم شهودا اذ تفيضون به

109. S. X, 61.

110. ما قلت لهم الا ما امرتوبه ان اعبدوا الله ربى وربكم وكنت عليهم شهيدا ما دمت فيهم، فلما توفيتنى كنت انت الرقيب عليهم وانت على كل شئ شهيد.

111. S. V. 117. 112. انت الرقيب عليهم

113. كان الله على كل شئ رقيبا 114. S. XXXIII, 52.

115. ان الله كان عليكم رقيبا 116. S. IV, 1.

117. سنريهم آياتنا فى الافاق وفى انفسهم حتى يتبين لهم انه الحق،
اولم يكف بربك انه على كل شىء شهيد الا انهم فى مرية
من لقاء ربهم، الا انه بكل شئ محيط

118. S. XLI, 53, 54.

119. هو الاول والاخر والظاهر والباطن وهو بكل شئ عليم

120. S. LVII, 3.

اول وآخر توی، کیست حدوث عدم
ظاہر و باطن توی چیست وجود وعدم
اول بے انتقال، آخر بے ارتحال
ظاہر بے چند وچون، باطن بے کیف وکم

122. انت الاول فليس قبلك شئ وانت الاخر فليس بعدك
شئ وانت الظاهر فليس فوقك شئ وانت الباطن فليس دونك شئ

123. وهو بكل شئ عليم

124. وقد خلقتك من قبل ولم تك شيئا 125. S. XIX, 9.

126. كان الله ولم يكن شئ قبله (رواه البخاري) 127. Bukhari.

128. ان الله على كل شئ شهيد

130. ما رأيت شيئا الا رأيت الله قبله

131. روے تو ظاہر است بعالم نہان کجاست
گر او نہان بود جہان خود عیان کجاست

132. افمن هو قائم على كل نفس بما كسبت (S. XIII, 33)

133. كان الله بكل شئ محيطا

134. وهو على كل شئ شهيد

135. هو الاول والآخر والظاهر والباطن

136. اولی وہم در اول آخری
باطنی وہم دوراں دم ظاہری
تو محیطی یرہمہ اندر صفات
وازہمہ پاکی و مستغنی بذات

137. وکیف ینکرالعشق ما فی الوجود الاھو !   138. Iraqi.

139. ھوالاول والاخر

140. عن ابی ھریرہ : والذی نفس محمد بیدہ لوانکم دلیتم
بجبل الی الارض السفلی لھبط علی اللہ ، ثم قراء : ھوالاول والاخر
والظاھر والباطن وھوبکل شئ علیم (رواہ احمد ترمذی)

141. ثم اللہ فوق ذلك

142. الرحمن علی العرش استوی   143. S. XX, 5.

144. ھواللہ فی السموات والارض   145. S. VI, 3.

146. نظر بر ہر چہ افگندیم واللہ   نیاید در نظر ما را جز اللہ

147. در عالم یا غیر او خیال است   مشو جانان گرفتار خیالات

148. & 149. See pages 3-6 above.

150. الاکل شی ما خلا اللہ باطل (لبید)

151. Abu Hureyra narrates that the Prophet said that the best words which the Arab poets had ever chanted were "Beware-etc".

152. خلق السموات والارض بالحق تعالی عما یشرکون

153. S. XVI, 3.   154. وتعالی اللہ ملك الحق

155. S. XX, 114.   156. وما خلقناھما الا بالحق

157. XLIV, 30.

158. ماخلق اللہ ذلك الا بالحق یفصل الآیات لقوم یعلمون (پ۱۱ ع ۶)

159. S. X, 6.

160. خلق الله السموات والارض بالحق ان فی ذالک لایۃً للمومنین

161. S. XXIX, 44. 162. هو الظاهر

163. ان الله هو الحق المبین 164. S. XXIV, 25.

165. الله نور السموات والارض 166. S. XXIV, 35.

167. یهدی الله لنوره من یشاء 168. S. XXIV, 35.

169. هو الاول والاخر والظاهر والباطن وهو بکل شیء علیم

170. S. LVII, 3.

171. وہی وجود منزہ بانزاہت خود
ہوا ہے جلوہ نما باشباہت ہر شئے

172. تراز دوست بگویم حکایت بے پوست
ہمہ از دوست وگر نیک بنگری ہمہ اوست
جمالش از ہمہ ذرات کون مکشوف است
حجاب تو ہمہ پندار ہائے تو بر تو است

173. وما یعقلها الا العالمون 174. S. XXIX, 43.

175. فهو (حق) مراتك فی رویتك نفسك وانت مراته فی رویة اسمائه وظهور احکامها.

176. اعیان ہمہ آئنہ وحق جلوہ گراست
یا نور بود آئنہ واعیان صوراست
در چشم محقق کہ حدید البصراست
ہریک دو ازیں آئنہ آئنہ دگراست

177. ظہور تو بمن است ووجود من از تو
فلست تظہر لولای لم اکن لولاک

178. فلولاه ولولانا فما كان الذى كانا

179. فوجودنا به وظهوره بنا

180 من وسع الحق فما ضاق عن

خلق فكيف الامر يا سامع

181. I am here referring to my Pir, the late Hadrat Muhammad Husain.

182. الحق منزه والحق مشبه

183. فلما تجلى ربه للجبل جبله دكا وخر موسى صعقا

184. S. VII, 143.

185. نودى من شاطى الواد الايمن فى البقعه المباركة من الشجرة

ان يا موسى انى انا الله رب العالمين .

186. S. XXVIII, 30.

187. يوم يكشف الساق ويدعون الى السجود

188. S. LXVIII, 42.

189. اذا كان يوم القيمة اذن ليتبع كل امة ما كانت تعبدون

فلا يبقى احد كان يعبد غير الله من الاصنام والانصاب الا يتا

قطون فى النار حتى لم يبق الا من يعبد الله من بر و فاجرا تاهم

رب العالمين، قال ماذا تنظرون ؟ يتبع كل امة ما كانت

تعبد - قالوا يا ربنا فارقنا الناس فى الدنيا افقر ما كنا اليهم و لم

نصاحبهم (و فى رواية ابى هريرة : فيقولون هذا مكاننا حتى ياتينا

ربنا فاذا جاء ربنا عرفناه) ، فيقول هل بينكم وبينه آية فعرفونه؟

فيقولون نعم ! فيكشف عن ساق الخ .

190. فيتمثل الرب تبارك تعالى فياتيهم (من حديث عبد الله بن

مسعود رضى الله عنه)

191. S. Hadith 'Abdulla Bin Mas'ud.

192. ویمثل لهم اشباہ ما کانوا یعبدون 193. Baihaqi

194. فیتجلی لهم فیغشاهم من نورہ 195. فیتجلی لنا ضاحکا

196. اذا تجلی بنورہ الذی ھو نورہ وقد رأی ربه مرتین

197. قال رسول الله صلعم رأیت ربی عزوجل فی احسن صورۃ

قال فیما یختصم الملأ الاعلی ؛ قلت انت اعلم . قال فوضع کفه بین

کتفی فوجدت بردھا بین ثدی فعلمت ما فی السموات والارض

وتلی ۔ کذلك نری ابراهیم ملکوت السموات والارض ولیکون

من الموقنین

198. S. VI, 76. 199. فاذا تبارك وتعالی فی احسن صورۃ

200. انی رأیت ربی فی احسن صورۃ شباب امرد

201. نص قطعی ہے حق تعالی کا تری صورت سے جلوہ گر ہونا

202. S. IV, 150.

203. کل شیء ھالك إلا وجهه 204. S. XXVIII, 88.

205. فان قلت بالتنزیه کنت مقیدا

وان قلت بالتشبیه کنت محددا

206. وان قلت بالامرین کنت مسددا

وکنت اماما فی المعارف سیدا

207. متحد بودیم بہ شاہ وجود

حکم غیریت بکلی محو بود

208. معلوم خدا ازل غیر خدا است ،

209. معرفت کی ہوائیں اُڑنے کو

عینیت غیریت در پر ہونا

210. عینیت سے مست ہوں اور غیریت سے ہوشیار

دم بدم یہ مے کشی یہ پارسائی بس مجھے

211. مرج البحرین یلتقیان بینهما برزخ لایبغیان فبای الاء ربکما تکذبان ؟

212. S. LX, 19, 20, 21.

213. ع ۔ نامے ست برمن زمن باقی اوست

214. اللہ غنی وانتم الفقراء 215. S. XLVII, 38.

216. یا ایها الناس انتم الفقراء الی اللہ واللہ هو الغنی الحمید

217. S. XXXV, 15.

218. ان الحکم الا للہ 219. S. VI, 57.

220. ولم یکن له شریك فی الملك 221. S. XVII, 111.

222. له مافی السموات ومافی الارض 223. S. X, 68.

224. وخلقکم و ما تعملون (S. XXXVII, 96)

225. جعلوا للہ شرکاء خلقوا کخلقه فتشابه الخلق علیهم، قل اللہ خالق کل شئ وهو الواحد القهار.

226. S. XIII, 16.

227. هو الحی القیّوم 228. S. II, 254.

229. وهو العلیم القدیر 230. S. XXX, 54.

231. ماتشاؤن الا ان یشاء اللہ 232. S. LXXVI, 30.

233. وانه هو السمیع البصیر 234. S. XVII, 1.

235. ہیچ می دانی کہ تو کیستی و چیستی

در دلت دریاب نیکو هستی یا نیستی

آنکہ می بیند بصیر است وآنکہ می شنود سمیع

آنکہ می داند علیم است خود بگو تو کیستی

236. اللہ لا الہ الا ھو الحی القیوم   237. S. II, 255.

238. ھو الاول والآخر والظاھر والباطن

239. S. LXII, 3.

240. میرا مجھ میں کچھ بھی نہیں سب ہے ترا
ترا تجھ کو دینے کیا جاتا ہے میرا

241. چیست توحید خدا آموختن
خویشتن را پیش واحد سوختن
گر ہمی خواہی کہ بفروزی چو روز
ہستی چو شمع شب خود را بسوز
زانکہ ہستی سخت مستی آورد
عقل از سر شرم از دل می برد
ہر کہ از ہستی خود مفقود شد
منتہائے کار او محمود شد

242. عاری حیات و علم سوں بے قدرت و بے خواست ہوں
احوال اپنا کیا کہوں میں نیں ہوں حق موجود ہے
میں ہوں اصم شنوا ہے حق، میں بے بصر، بینا ہے حق
میں گنگ ہو گویا ہے حق، میں نیں ہوں حق موجود ہے
اول بھی حق آخر بھی حق، باطن بھی حق ظاہر بھی حق
غائب بھی حق حاضر بھی حق، میں نیں ہوں حق موجود ہے
ذاتی صفت حق کی قِدَم میری حقیقت ہے عدم
لحظہ بہ لحظہ دم بدم میں نیں ہوں حق موجود ہے
تھا حق نہ تھا میں اولا نہ رہوں گا مستقبلا
الآن کما کان کو سن میں نیں ہوں حق موجود ہے

243. سبحان الله وما انا من المشرکین 244. S. XII, 108.

245. تو بہ قیمت دارا ے ہر دو جہانی
چہ کنم قدر خود نمی دانی

246. ما جام جہاں نمائے ذاتیم
ما مظہر جملہ صفاتیم
ہم صورت واجب الوجودیم
ہم معنی جملہ ممکناتیم
برتر زمکان و در مکانیم
برون زجہات و در جہاتیم
بیمار و ضعیف را شفائم
محبوس و نحیف را نجاتیم
چون قطب زجاے خود نجبیم
چون چرخ اگرچہ بے ثباتیم

247. مائم ستون و سقف مینا
مائم مدار جملہ اشیاء
مائم محیط و مرکز و دور
پرکار وجود بر ہمہ طور
سلطان سریر قاب قوسین
مائم و طفیل ماست کونین

248. وجودنا منه وقیامنا به ؛ هو ولا غیره وکلا له
دی گفت کہ اے عاشق شیدا تا تو
یکتا شدی از دوی یکم ام با تو

دیدم او را بچشم او پس گفتم
اے جان جہان تو کیستی؟ گفتا تو
گفتمش خواہم کہ بینم مر ترا اے نازنین
گفت خواہی گر مرا بینی برو خود را ببین
گفتمش با تو نشستن آرزو دارد دلم
گفت گر این آرزو باشد ترا با خود نشین
گفتمش بے پردہ با تو گر سخن گویم رواست
گفت در پردہ نشاید گفت با ما بیش ازین

249. الا بذکر اللہ تطمئن القلوب

250. S. XIII, 29.

251. کاے بلبل جان مست بیاد تو مرا
وے پا بہ غم پست بیاد تو مرا
لذات جہاں راہمہ در پا فگند
ذوقی کہ دہد دست بیاد تو مرا

252. Lawaih, Flash XI, Trans. by Whinfield.

در ہجر تو بودہ اندوہ و آزارم
از وصل تو رفت ہستی و پندارم
شادی آمد و نصیب جانم شد
اکنوں جان و تن خویش را براحت دارم

یا ایها النفس المطمئنه ترجعی الی ربك راضیة مرضیه'
فادخلی فی عبادی وادخلی جنتی

254. S. LXXXIX, 27-30.

255. یضل من یشاء ویهدی من یشاء

256. S. LXXIV, 31.

257. چون ذات تو منفی بود اے صاحب جش
از نسبت افعال بخودش باش خمش
شیریں مثلے شنو، مکن روے ترش
ثبت العرش اولاثم انقش

258. Lawa'ih, Flash XXVI, Trans. by Whinfield.

259. هر کجا می نگرد دیده درو می نگرد
هر چه می بینم از وجمله باو می بینم
تو زیکسو نظر می کن ومن از همه سو
تو زیکسو منش از همه سو می بینم
گاه به جمله وگه جمله ازو می بینم
گاه او جمله وگه جمله ازو می بینم
مغربی این که تواش می طلبی در خلوت
من عیان بر سر هر کوچه وکو می بینم

260. فلا تنظر العین الا الیه
ولا یقع الحکم الا علیه
فنحن له وبه فی یدیه
وفی کل حال فانا لدیه

261. اللهم انی اسألك لذة النظر الی وجهك وشوقا الی لقاءك فی
غیر ضراء مضرة ولا فتنة مضلة (رواه النسائی).

262. Nisai'.

263. لکیلا تاسوا علی مافاتکم ولا تفرجوا بما اتاکم

264. S. LVII, 23.

265. اے که شب وروز خدا می طلبی
کوری اگر از خونشین جدا می طلبی

حق باتو بهر زبان سخن می گوید
سر تا قدمت منم کجا می طلبی ؟
264. ای آن که خدا می بجوئی هر جا
تو عین خدائی نه جدائی بخدا
این جستن تو بدان می ماند
که قطره میان آب و می جوید دریا
265. ای دوست ترا بهر مکان می جستم
هر دم خبرت زاین و آن می جستم
دیدم بتو خویش را تو خود من بودی
خجلت زده ام کز تو نشان می جستم
ای دوست میان ما جدائی تا کے
چوں من توام این توی و مای تا کے
با غیرت تو مجال غیرے چو نماند
پس در نظر این غیر نمای تا کے
266. ماند آن الله باقی جمله رفت
الله لیس فی الوجود غیر الله
267. خیال کج ہمیں باین جا و شناس
ھر کہ در خدا گم شد خدا نیست

268. قل الله ثم ذرهم 269. S. VI, 92.

270. لی مع الله وقت لا یمسی فیه ملك مقرب او نبی مرسل

271. سبحان الذی اسری بعبده 272. S. XVII, 1.

273. فاوحی الی عبده ما اوحی 274. S. LIII, 10.

با ہمہ قربیکہ دارد با خدا
از ریاضت نیست یکدم او جدا
زانکہ ہر کو مقتدائے راہ شد
وز بد و نیک جہان آگاہ شد
گر نباشد در عمل ثابت قدم
چو رہاند خلق را از دست غم
مقتدا چوں در ریاضت قائم است
تا بش را میل طاعت دائم است
دیگر آنکہ شان حق بے غایت است
ہر زمانش نوع دیگر آیت است
چونکہ معروف است بیحد لاجرم
معرفت بے غایت آمد نیز ہم
عمرہا گر او ریاضت می کند
روز شب را صرف طاعت می کند
دم بدم بیند جمال دیگر او
لاجرم دائم بود در جستجو
حال پیغمبر نگر با این کمال
فاستقم بودش خطاب از ذوالجلال
رہنمائی لائق آن کامل است
کز خودی فانی بجانان واصل است
رہبر راہِ طریقت آن بود
کو باحکام شریعت می رود

این چنین کامل بجو گر ره روی
تا ز وصل دوست با بهره شوی
276. زانکه گر جاے نظر خواهی فگند
در کنار خویش سر خواهی فگند
کیست زو بهتر بگو اے ہیچ کس
تا بدان دل شاد باشی یک نفس
من نه شادی خواهم و نے خسروی
آنچه می خواهم من از تو هم توی
277. از زندگیم بندگئ تست ہوس
بر زنده دلان بے تو حرام است نفس
خواهد ز تو مقصود دل خود ہر کس
جامی ز تو بس ترا می خواهد و بس
278. الٰهی انت مقصودی ورضاءك مطلوبی، ترکت لك الدنیا
والآخرة ، اتمم علیّ نعمتك وارزقنی وصولك التام
279. فروح وریحان وجنت نعیم
280. S. LVI, 89.

CHAPTER IV

خود را بشیون ذات آن پرده نشین
شد جلوه ده از مظاهره دنیی و دین
زین نکته که گفتم اے طلب گار یقین
ذات و صفت و فعل و اثر چیست ببین

2. Lawaih, P. 41, Trans. by E.H. Whinfield.

3. چون حق بتفاصیل شیون گشت عیان
مشهود شد این عالم پر سود و زیان
گر باز روند عالم و عالمیان
با رتبہ اجمال حق آید عیان

4. Ibid, Flash XXV.

5. Junayd.

6. Shaykh Akbar in Fusus.

7. اللہ ھوالوجود الحق

8. وجود بالمعنی المصدری

9. وجود بالمعنی للوجود

ہستی بقیاس وعقل اصحاب قیود
جز عارض اعیان وحقائق نہ نمود
لیکن بمکاشفات ارباب شہود
اعیان ہمہ عارض اند معروض وجود

12. Lawaih, Flash XIV.

13. لیس کمثلہ شیٔ

14. ہرچند کہ جان عارف آگاہ بود
کے در حرم قیس تواش راہ بود
دست ہمہ اہل کشف وارباب شہود
از دامن ادراک تو کوتاہ بود

15. Lawa'ih, Flash XXVI Trans. by E.H. Whinfield.

16. العجزعن درك الادراك ادراك

17. In the works of most of the early and late writers, the learned scholars (such as Imam Ghazzali, Muhyid Din-ibn-ul 'Arabi, Shaykh Abdu'l-Karim Jili, Shah 'Abdu'l-'Aziz and Shah Abdu'l Haqq) have stated that this is a quotation from Abu Bakr Siddiq.

18. انچه پیش تو پیش ازان ره نیست
غایت فهم تست اللہ نیست

19. لا یعرف الله الا الله

20. وحدت

21. واحدیت

22. This table is reproduced from Maulana Ashraf 'Ali Thanawi's book 'Kitab al-Takashuf'.

23. Jili—Insan-i-Kamil (Cairo) Vol. I, q. 43, Translated by J. W. Sweetman.

24. کان الله ولم یکن معه شئ

25. ولا یحیطون به علما

26. S. XX, 10.

27. یحذرکم الله نفسه

28. S. III, 30.

29. ماعرفناك حق معرفتك

30. لاتفکروا فی الله فتهلکوا

31. در ذات خدا فکر فراوان چه کنی
جان را ز قصور خویش حیران چه کنی
چون تو نه رسی به کنه یک ذره تمام
در کنهٔ خدا دعوئ عرفان چه کنی

32. کل الناس فی ذات اللہ حمقاء

33. عنقا شکار کس نشود دام باز چین

کانجا ہمیشہ باد بدست است دام را

34. The following quotation has been ascribed to Dhu'l Num al Misri :

العلم فی ذات الحق جهل والكلام فی حقيقة المعرفة حيرة

والاشارة عن المشير شرك

'Knowledge of the Essence of God is ignorance, description of the essence of gnosis is Stupefaction and any indication from an indicator is association of others with God as coequals (Shirk).'

35. انچہ در ذاتش تفکر کردنیست

در حقیقت آں نظر در ذات نیست

ہست آن پندار او زیرا براہ

صد ہزاراں پردہ آمد تا الہ

36 Cf - Introduction to Fusus-'l-Hikam by Shah Mubarak 'Ali printed at Muktba-i Ahmadi, Kanpur, pp. 53, 54.

37. لقد كفر الذين قالوان الله هو المسيح ابن مريم

(۱) اول ما خلق الله للعقل

(۲) اول ما خلق الله نوری

(۳) اول ما خلق الله روحی

38. S. V. 19.

39. & 40. Though this tradition is not cited in the books of Traditions textually, it is correct according to the sense. Therefore 'Abdur Razzaq has quoted the authority from Jabir bin-'Abdulla himself who states that once the Prophet Muhammad said:

ان الله خلق قبل الاشياء نور نبيك من نوره فجعل ذلك
النور يدور بالقدرة حيث يشاء، ولم يكن ذلك الوقت
لوح ولا قلم ولا جنة ولا نار ولا سماء ، ولا ملك
ولا ارض ولا شمس ولا قمر ولا جن ولا جان . فلما
اراد الله ان يخلق الخلق قسم ذلك النور باربعة اجزاء
فخلق من الجزء الاول القلم، من الثانى اللوح ،من
الثالث العرش ، ثم قسم الجزء الرابع اربعة اجزاء •

"God Created the light of our Prophet before He Created other things. He let that light revolve wherever it liked. At that time there was neither the Table, nor the Pen, nor Heaven, nor Hell, nor angels, nor sky, nor earth, nor the Sun, nor the moon, nor jinn, nor animal. When God intended to Create the world, He divided the Light into four parts. From the first He Created the pen, from the second, the Table, from the third, the Throne. He then divided the fourth part into four further parts."

41. قل هو الله احد

والهکم الہ واحد لا الہ الا ھوالرحمن الرحیم

43. S. II, 163.

44. Printed at Abu'l'Ulai Press, Hyderabad-Deccan (India), pp. 33-34.

45. اے درہمہ شان ذات تو پاک از ہمہ شین
نے درحق توکیف تو ان گفت نہ این
از روے تعقل ہمہ غیراند صفات
با ذات تو از روے تحقق ہمہ عین

46. Lawa'ih, Flash XV, translated by E.H. Whinfield.

47. Weber's History of Philosophy, translated by Thilly, p. 331.

48. الاعیان الثابتۃ ماشمت رائحۃ الوجود

49. اعیان بحضیض عین ناکردہ نزول
حاشاکہ بود بجعل جاعل مجعول
چون جعل بود افاضۂ نور وجود
توصیف عدم بآن نباشد معقول

50. قل کل یعمل علی شاکلتہ

51. S. XVII, 84.

52. الم تر الی ربك کیف مد الظل

53. S. XXV, 45.

54. اعیان ہمہ آئینہ وحق جلوہ گر است

55. This alone is the mystery of creation. It has been explained in the 3rd Chapter above.

Therefore it has been presented here briefly.

56. عدم آئینۂ ہستی است مطلق

کز و پیدا است عکسِ تابش حق

عدم چون گشت ہستی را مقابل

درو عکسے شد اندر حال حاصل

شد آن وحدت ازیں کثرت پدیدا

یکے را چون شمردی گشت بسیار

عدد گرچہ یکے دارد بدایت

ولیکن ہرگزش نبودہ نہایت

عدم در ذات خود چوں بود صافی

ازو باظاہر آمد گنج مخفی

حدیث کنت کنزاً را فرو خوان

کہ تا پیدا بہ بینی سر پنہاں

57. *Gulshan-i-Raz, II. 133-139. Translated by E.H. Whinfield.*

58. كنت كنزاً مخفيا فاحببت ان اعراف فخلقت الخلق لاعرف

59. Hafiz Sakhawi has copied this Tradition in Maqasid-i-Hasna with the addition and omission of some words and the great scholar Traditionist Muhammad bin Ibrahim has said, "This tradition is narrated by the Sufis and

he who ponders over the following verse of the Qur'an has to acknowledge the validity of this tradition:

الذی خلق سبع سموات ومن الارض مثلهن یتنزل الامر بینهن لتعلموا ان اللہ علی کل شئ قدیر و ان اللہ احاط بکل شئ علما

"Allah it is Who hath created seven heavens, and of the earth like thereof; the commandment cometh down among them slowly, that he may know that Allah is Able to do all things, and that Allah surroundeth everything in Knowledge (S. LXV, 12) Mulla 'Ali. Qari says that the meaning of this tradition is in accordance with the following assertion of God Almighty:

وما خلقت الجن والانس الا لیعبدون

"I created the jinn and humankind only that they might worship me"

60. For further explanation vide Chapter III.

61. از محبت گشت ظاہر ہر چہ ہست
وا ز محبت می نماید نیست ہست
ناز معشوقی بہ تقاضاے نیاز
کرد پیدا تا نماید جملہ راز

از نیاز ماست ناز او عیان

61. می کند اجبت این معنی بیان

آنکہ معشوق ست از وجہ کرد

عاشقش می گو اگر داری خبر

62. ان اللہ غنی عن العالمین

64. دامان غنائے مطلق پاک آمد پاک

از آلودگی نیاز ما مشتے خاک

چون جلوہ گر و نظارگی جملہ خود اوست

گر ما و تو درمیان نباشیم چہ باک

66. آئنہ ساخت عالم و خود را بخود دید

عکس و جمال اوست نہان و عیان کہ ہست

چون حسن او بنقش جہان کرد جلوہ

ظاہر نمود این ہمہ کون و مکان کہ ہست

کو نام و کو نشان زغیر و کجاست غیر

یار است ظاہر از ہمہ نام و نشان کہ ہست

67. آن یار عین است نہ از روے اتحاد

این خانہ پر است ولیکن نہ از حلول

دانش ہمہ بہ مذہب ماہست معرفت

در دین ما جز این نہ فروع است نہ اصول

68. زعم باطل کی تجہ کو مستی کب تک

ناداں یہ ادعاے ہستی کب تک

تو بھی موجود اور حق بھی موجود

ظالم یہ شرک و خود پرستی کب تک

69. من عرف نفسه فقد عرف ربه

70. جوہرے جز خودشناسی نیست در بحر وجود

ماںگرد خویش می گردیم چون گرداب ہا

71. ہمسایہ و ہم نشین و ہمرہ ہمہ اوست

در دلق گدا و اطلس شہ ہمہ اوست

در انجمن فرق و نہان خانہ جمع

باللہ ہمہ اوست ثم باللہ ہمہ اوست

72. Lawaih, Flash XXII

73. علم یقین گشتہ حق یقین

کردم این نکتہ را ازان تضمین

کہ ہمہ اوست ہر چہ ہست یقین

جاں و جاناں و دلبر و دل و دین

74. بر سر این و آں ناز دہ خط

پندار دوی دلیل بعد است و سخط

در جملہ کائنات بے سہو و غلط

یک عین فحسب داں و یک ذات فقط

75. Lawaih, Flash XXV

76. غیر یک ذات در دو عالم کو؟

لیس فی الکائنات الا ہو!

77. از رہ صورت نماید غیر دوست
چون نظر کردی بمعنی جملہ اوست
زاں یکے ماعندکم ینفد شنو
جزپے ماعندنا باق مرو
78. ماعندکم ینفد
79. ماعندنا باق
80. S. XVI, 96.
81. گر طالب شر بود وگر کاسب خیر
گر صاحب خانقہ وگر راہب دیر
از روے تعین ہمہ غیر اند نہ عین
وز روے حقیقت ہماں عین اند نہ غیر
82. جز یک رہ نیست پیوستہ بہ کل
ورنہ خود باطل بدے بعث برسل
چون رسولان از پے پیوستن اند
پس چہ پیوندند آں چوں یک تن اند
83. من نیم جنس شہنشہ دور ازو
لیک دارم در تجلی نور ازو
84. از ہمہ در صفات وذات جدا
لیس شئ کمثلہ ابدا
85. اے بردہ گمان کہ صاحب تحقیقی
وندر صفت صدق ویقین صدیقی

هر مرتبه از وجود حکمے دارد
گر حفظ مراتب نہ کنی زندیقی

86. Lawaih Flash XXIII Trans. by E.H. Whinfield

87. الفقر اذا تمّ هو الله

88. Seemingly a Hadith. Poverty, utter annihilation of self (Gulshan-i-Raz), 1, 128.

89. معشوق و عشق و عاشق هر سہ یک است اینجا
چون وصل نگنجد ہجران چہ کار دارد

90. واعبد ربك حتى يأتيك اليقين

91. S. XV, 99.

92. هو انقطاع الخاطر عن تعلق ماسوى الله تعالى بالكليه

93. کہ بستگان کمند تو رستگارانند (حافظ)

94. خواجگی را خواجگی از بندگی است
بندگی کردن کمال خواجگی است
من ازان روز کہ بند تو ام آزادم
پادشاہم کہ بدست تو اسیر افتادم

95. انا عبدك 96. من رانی فقد رأی الحق

97. Bukhari & Muslim.

CHAPTER V

1. مرید : اے شریک ہستی خاصاں بدر
میں نہیں سمجھا حدیث جبر و قدر
پیر : بال بازان راسوے سلطان برد
بال زاغان را بہ گورستان برد

2. Ethics, Part III Prop. II, Note. 2 . Prop. XXXV, Note.

3. اذا ذكر القدر فامسكوا (طبراني عن ابن مسعود

4. لا تكلّموا في القدر فانه سر الله فلا تفشوا الله سره (ابونعيم في الحلية)

5. ان في ذلك لذكرى لمن كان له قلب او القى
السمع وهو شهيد

6. S. L. 37

7. القدر من اجل العلوم وما يفهم الله تعالى الا لمن اختصه
الله بالمعرفة التامة

8. انا كل شئ خلقنا بقدر ...... وكل شئ فعلوه في الزبر

9. S. LIV. 49, 52.

10. الله خالق كل شئ .S. XIII, 163

11. S. XXXVII,13. والله خلقكم وما تعملون

12. ام جعلوا الله شركاء وخلقوا كخلقه فتشابه الخلق عليهم، قل الله
خالق كل شئ وهو الواحد القهار (سورة رعد، ١٦)

13. والله خلقکم وما تعملون

14. می شناسی طبع ادراک از کجا است

حورے اندر بنگہ خاک از کجا است

طاقت فکر حکیمان از کجا است

قوت فکر حکیمان از کجا است

این دل واین واردات از کیست

این فنون و معجزات از کیست

گرمی گفتار داری از تو نیست

شعلہ کردار داری از تو نیست

این ہمہ فیض از بہار فطرت است

فطرت از پروردگار فطرت است

15. یا رسول اللہ أرأیت ما نعمل فیہ علی امر قد فرغ منہ او امر
نبتد أفقال علی امر قد فرغ منہ، فقال عمر افلا نتکل
وندع العمل، فقال اعملوا فکل میسر لما خلق لہ

16. الآن طاب العمل

17. ارأیت رقی نسترقیہا ودواء نتداوی بہ ھل یرد من قدر اللہ
تعالی فقال انہ من قدر اللہ

18. لا یؤمن احدکم حتی یومن بالقدر خیرہ شرہ من اللہ تعالی

19. الخلق من اللہ

20. کسب

21. S. II, 286. لا یکلف اللہ نفسا الا وسعھا لھا ما کسبت
وعلیھا ما اکتسبت

22. ان احسنتم احسنتم لانفسکم وان اسأتم فلھا

23. ان اللہ لا یطاع باکراہ ولا یعصی بغلبۃ ولم یھمل
العباد من المملکۃ

24. S. II, 256. لا اکراہ فی الدین

25. ان اللہ لا یقوی الابرار بالجبر وانما قواھم بالیقین

26. کافر

27. فاجر

28. من لم یؤمن بالقدر فقد کفر ومن احالی المعاصی علی
اللہ فقد فجر

29. بپاے خود مزن زنجیر تقدیر
تہ این گنبد گردون رہے ہست
اگر باور نداری خیز و دریاب
کہ چون پا واکنی جولانگہے است

30. ارضیان نقد خودی درباختند
نکتہ تقدیر را نشناختند
رمز باریکش بہ حرفے مضمر است
تو اگر دیگر شوی او دیگر است
خاک شو نذر ہوا سازد ترا
سنگ شو بر شیشہ اندازد ترا

شبنمی افگند گی تقدیرتست

قلزمی پایند گی تقدیرتست

31. الاعیان الثابتة

32. شاکله

33. قابلیت به جعل جاعل نیست فعل فاعل خلاف قابل نیست

34 لیس کمثله شئ هوالسمیع البصیر

35. S. LII, 11.

36. خلقکم وما تعملون

37. لا یمکن لعین ان یظهر فی الوجود ذاتا صفة و فعلا
الآ بقدر خصوصیة واصلیته واستعداد الذاتی

لاحول ولاقوة الا بالله

ما یحکم علینا الا بنا بل نحن نحکم علینا بنا

42. اتاکم من کل ما سألتموه

41. S. XIV, 34.

43. انا لموفوهم نصیبهم غیرمنقوص

44. S. XI, 109. 45. S. VI, 150. فلله الحجة البالغة

46. هرچه از زین وشین شما است

برسر مقتضاے عین شما است

هرچه عین شما تقاضا کردو

جودِ فیض من آن هویدا کرد

47. اے عین تو نسخہ کتاب اول
مشروع دران صحیفہ اسرار ازل
احکام قضا چو بود درو بدرج
حق کرد باحکام کتاب تو عمل

48. حق عالم و اعیانِ خلائق معلوم
معلوم بود حاکم و عالم محکوم
برموجب حکم تو کند با تو عمل
گر تو بمثل معذبی ور مرحوم

49. يداك كسبتا وفوك نفخ

50. Shaykh Akbar.

51. وما اصابكم من مصيبة فيما كسبت ايدكم

52. S. XLII, 30.

53. خلق كل شئ وقدّره تقديرا

54. ان الحق لايعطيه الاما اعطاه عينه

55. خودی کو کر بلند اتنا کہ ہر تقدیر سے پہلے
خدا بندے سے خود پوچھے بتا تیری رضا کیا ہے

56. تقدیر شکن قوت باقی ہے ابھی اس میں
نادان جسے کہتے ہیں تقدیر کا زندانی

57. الخلق من الحق والكسب من الخلق

58. لاجبر ولاقدر بل الامر بين الامرين

59. بشنو سخن مشکل و سِرِّ مغلق

هر فعل و صفت کہ باشد باعیان ملحق

از یک نسبت آن جملہ مضاف است بما

از وجہ دیگر جملہ مضاف است بحق

60. Lawaih, Flash XXX, Trans. by E.H. Whinfield.

61. جبر باشد پرّ و بال کاملان

جبر ہم زندان و بند جاہلان

بال بازان راسوے سلطان برد

بال زاغان را بہ گورستان برد

CHAPTER VI

1 هر نسبت که از قبیل خیر است و کمال
باشد ز نعوت پاک متعال
هر وصف که در حساب شر است و وبال
دارد به قصور قابلیات مآل

2. Lawa'ih, Flash XXVII, Translated by E.H. Whinfield.

3. هر جا که وجود کرده سیر است اے دل
می دان به یقین که خیر است اے دل
هر شر ز عدم بود عدم غیر وجود
پس شر همه مقتضاے غیر است اے دل

4. گر آمدیم بمن بدے نامدمے
ور نیز شدن بمن بدے کے شدمے

5. نه زین نبدی که اندرین درین خراب
نے آمدمے نے شدمے نے بدمے

6. The Rubaiyat of Omar Khayyam, done into English by Edward Fitz Gerald. Quatrain XXXII

7. J.S. Mill: Three Essays on Religion (Henry Holt Company, "Nature" pp 3—69.

اسرار وجود خام و آشفته بماند
وان گوهر بس شریف ناسفته بماند
هر کس ز سرِ قیاس حرفی گفتند
وان نکته که اصل بود ناگفته بماند

9. نفی آن یک چیز و اثباتش رواست
چون جهت شد مختلف نسبت دوتاست

10. وهو العليم القدير

11. S. XXX, 54

12. الا يعلم من خلق وهو اللطيف الخبير

13. S. LXVII, 14.

14. وهو بكل خلق عليم

15. S. XVI, 78.

16. افغير الله تتقون

17. S. XVI, 52.

The Living, the Self-subsisting, Eternal! (S. II, 245).

18. هو الحی القيوم

19. هو الحی القنوم

20. وهو العليم القدير

21. وهو العليم القدير

22. وانه هو السميع البصير

23.

25. کے دہد دست جعل جاعل را
که موافق کند قوابل را

26. نہان بصورت اغیار یار پیدا شد
عیان بنقش و نگار آن نگار پیدا شد
پدید گشت ز کثرت جمال وحدت او
یکے بکثرت چندین ہزار پیدا شد

27. خلق السموات والارض بالحق ان فی ذلک لایة للمومنین

28. S. XXIX, 41. 29. ان الله هو الحق المبین

30. S. XXIV, 25.

31. الله نور السموات والارض

32. S. XXIV, 35.

33. ان الله جمیل ویحب الجمال

34 الوجود خیر محض والعدم شر بحت

35. ان الله جمیل لایصدر عنه الا جمیل

36. Hadrat Ali.

37. حقیقة الشئ لاتنفک عن الشئ

38. اعیان ہمہ شیشہ ہاے گوناگون بود
کافتادہ بران پرتوے خورشید وجود
ہر شیشہ کہ بود سرخ یا زرد و کبود
خورشید در آن ہم بہ ہمان رنگ نمود

39. ظہور تو بمن است و وجود من از تو
فلست تظہر لولای لم اکن لولاک

40. فوجودنا به ظهوره بنا

41. هر جا که وجود کرده سیر است اے دل
میدان به یقین که محض خیر است اے دل
هر شر ز عدم بود و عدم غیر وجود
پس شر همه مقتضائے غیر است اے دل

42. الوجود خیر والعدم شر

43. کل شئ یرجع الی اصله

44. الحسنات کلها من الوجود والسیئات کلها من العدم والفقود

45. الخیر کله فی یدیك والشر لیس الیك (مسلم)

46. Muslim.

47. ما اصابك من حسنة فمن الله وما اصابك من سیئة فمن نفسك

48. S. IV, 79.

50. هر نعت که از قبیل خیر است و کمال
باشد ز نعوت پاک متعال
هر وصف که در حساب شر است و وبال
دارد به قصور قابلیات مآل

51. والله خلقکم وما تعملون

52. ظاهر لنفسه ومظهر لغیره

53. الله نور السموات والارض

54. S. XXIV, 35.

55. قل کل من عند الله

56. S. X, 78.

56. کل خیر و شر من اللہ تعالی

57. واللہ خالق الجازر وجزورہ

58. والی اللہ ترجع الامور

59. S. II, 210.

60. ہر شر ز عدم بود و عدم غیر وجود

61. والشر لیس یعود الیك

62.

63. شپرہ با حضرت خورشید گفت
چشم را کور چرا می کنی
گفت ترا طاقت دیدار نیست
کور خودی شکوہ ز ما می کنی

1. اللهم انی اسئلك لذة النظر الی وجهك والشوق الی لقاءك فی
غیر ضراء مضرة ولا فتنه مضلة

2. Hadith Nisai.

3. والذین جاهدوا فینا لنهدینهم سُبلنا

4. S. XXIX, 69.

5. لکل درجات مما عملوا

6. S. VI. 132.

7. حب الدنیا راس کل خطیئة

8. هوالاول والآخر والظاهر والباطن وهوبکل شیء علیم

9. S. LVII, 3.

10. اے دل طلب کمال در مدرسه چند
تکمیل اصول وحکمت وهندسه چند
هر فکر که جز ذکر خدا وسوسه است
شرم زخدا بدار این وسوسه چند

11. Lawaih, Flash II, Trans. by Whinsfield.

12. کیست زو بهتر بگو اے هیچ کس
تا بدان دل شاد باشی یک نفس
من نه شادی خواهم و نے خسروی
آنچه من می خواهم از هم توی

13. سبحان الله وما انا من المشرکین

14. S. XII, 108.

15. انت الظاهر فلیس قبلك شئ

16. الحق محسوس والخلق معقول

17. ذوالعین 18. ما رأیتُ شیئاً اِلا رایتُ الله قبله

19. روے تو ظاہر است بعالم نہان کجاست
گر او نہان بود جہان خود عیان کجاست

20. ذوالعقل 21. الخلق محسوس والحق معقول

22. یاریست مرا ورائے پردہ — حسن رخ او سزائے پردہ
عالم ہمہ پردہ مصور — اشیاء ہمہ نقشہائے پردہ
این پردہ مرا ازتو جدا کرد — اینست خود اقتضائے پردہ

23. گوید کہ میان ما جدای — ہر گر نہ کند عطائے پردہ

24. از صفائی مے ولطافت جام — درہم آمیخت رنگ جام ومدام
ہمہ جام ست ونیست گوی مے — یا مدام است نیست گوی جام

25. Jami.

26. عینیت سے مست ہون اور غیریت سے ہوشیار
دم بدم یہ میکشی یہ پارسائی بس مجھے

27. ذوالعینی اگر نور حقت مشہود است
ذوالمعقلی اگر شہود حق مفقود است
ذوالعینی و ذوالعقلی شہود حق وخلق
بایک دگر از ہر دو ترا موجود است

Vide his peerlesswork.

28. Mizan-al-Tawhid: p. 146.

29 انت الظاهر فليس فوقك شئ

30. نیرنگیوں سے یار کے حیران نہ ہوجیو
ہر رنگ میں اسی کو نمودار دیکھنا

31. الفقر اذا تم ھو الله 32. میں نہیں ہوں حق موجود ہے

33. خود ہمو شاہد و ہمو مشہود
غیر او نیست در جہان موجود

34. ماند آن الله باقی جملہ رفت
الله لیس فی الوجود غیر الله

35. اندرین رہ می تراش و می خراش
تا دم آخر دمے فارغ مباش
تا دم آخر دمے آخر بود
کہ عنایت با تو صاحب سر بود
دوست دارد دوست این آشفتگی
کوشش بیہودہ بہ از خفتگی!
کارے کن و کاہل مباش
اندک اندک خاک چہ را می تراش
چون ز چاہے می کنی ہر روز خاک
عاقبت اندر رسی در آب پاک
چون نشینی بر سر کوے کسے
عاقبت بینی تو ہم روے کسے

36. لی مع اللہ وقت لا یسعنی فیہ ملك مقرب او نبی مرسل

37. & 38. ھو الظاھر

39. " "

40. رخ گرچہ نمی نمائم سال بسال

حاشا کہ بود، مہر ترا وہم زوال

41. Lawaih, Flash VII.

دارم ہمہ جا با ہمہ کس در ہمہ حال

در دل ز تو آرزو و در دیدہ خیال

41. خواہی کہ شوی داخلِ ارباب نظر

از قال بحال بایدت کرد گزر

از گفتن توحید موحد نشوی

شیریں نشود دہان بنام شکر

42. توحید حق اے خلاصہ مخترعات

باشد بہ سخن حق یافتن از ممتنعات

رو، نفی وجود کن کہ دریابی

چیزے کہ نیابی ز فصوص ولمعات

43. سبحان اللہ وما انا من المشرکین

44. ادعونی استجب لکم

45. S. XL, 60.

46. کفی باللہ وکیلا

47. S. IV, 81.

48. ان اللہ مع الصابرین

49. S. II, 150.

50. اسلمتُ لرب العالمین

51. S. II, 131.

52. والذین جاھدوا فینا لنھدینھم سبلنا

53. S. XXIX, 69.

54. ھوالظاھر

55. فاینما تولوا فثم وجہ اللہ

56. S. II, 115.

57. الذین آمنوا اشد حبا للہ

58. S. II, 165.

59. بعشق کوش چو عارف شدی بسر جمال

کہ عارفان ہمہ لب اندو عاشقانِ لب لب

60. اللھم انی اسئلك لذة النظ الی وجھك والشوق الی لقائك

61. فادخلی فی عبادی وادخلی جنتی

62. S. LXXXIX, 28.

63. عینا یشرب بالمقربون

64. S. LXXXIII, 64.

65. اللھم انی اسئلك نعیما لاینفد وقرة عین لاتنقطع

66. برد العیش فی الدنیا والاخرہ

67. S. II. 165.

تمت بالخیر

INDEX OF NAMES OF PERSONS AND PLACES

INDEX OF TECHNICAL TERMS

100 YEARS

मोतीलाल बनारसीदास
सैद मिठा
बाजार
लाहौर

1903

MOTILAL BA

PUBLI